J. R. C. Nicolls

Agricultural engineering in India

Irrigation

J. R. C. Nicolls

Agricultural engineering in India
Irrigation

ISBN/EAN: 9783741175626

Manufactured in Europe, USA, Canada, Australia, Japa

Cover: Foto ©Andreas Hilbeck / pixelio.de

Manufactured and distributed by brebook publishing software
(www.brebook.com)

J. R. C. Nicolls

Agricultural engineering in India

AGRICULTURAL
ENGINEERING IN INDIA.

IRRIGATION.

BY

J. R. C. NICOLLS,
EXECUTIVE ENGINEER, INDIAN P.W.D.

REPRINTED FROM "ENGINEERING."

LONDON:
OFFICES OF "ENGINEERING,"
35 & 36, BEDFORD STREET, STRAND, W.C.

Price 3s. 6d.

AGRICULTURAL

ENGINEERING IN INDIA.

IRRIGATION.

BY

J. R. C. NICOLLS,

EXECUTIVE ENGINEER, INDIAN P.W.D.

REPRINTED FROM "ENGINEERING."

LONDON:
OFFICES OF "ENGINEERING,"
35 & 36, BEDFORD STREET, STRAND. W.C.

AGRICULTURAL ENGINEERING IN INDIA.

INTRODUCTORY.

IN the following articles the writer has attempted to describe the work on which a large number of engineers are employed in India. This work is so different from what usually falls to the lot of civil engineers, that a description of it can scarcely fail to interest our readers.

The irrigation works of Northern India form one of the principal features of the country. They contribute most materially to its prosperity, and have an absorbing interest for those engaged on them. Yet, outside the departments immediately concerned, next to nothing is known of these works. The reason is not far to seek. The works are carried on by a staff of Government engineers. Their working life is spent in India. They have no engineering connection in England. No object in keeping their names and works before the public.

These works involve in their construction most of the engineering difficulties usually met with in railway or road making. They are intimately connected with the social life and welfare of the people, and form a most important factor in their commercial prosperity, depending, as they do, on agriculture for everything they possess. To their construction and maintenance, therefore, the term Agricultural Engineering is peculiarly applicable.

This term is not merely suited to the general principles on which the works are projected and designed ; but the term Agricultural Engineer adequately describes the officer who is employed on the maintenance of these works, who spends his life amongst the cultivators, cordially assisting them to improve the condition of their land and crops.

The writer proposes first to consider the numerous issues—geological, social, financial, and professional—which must be most critically entered into before undertaking an extensive irrigation scheme. The purely engineering questions involved in the carrying it out will then require our attention.

The following considerations are couched in general terms. They are applicable to irrigation schemes for any fairly flat alluvial country ; at the same time the writer has chosen to take as a subject for description and comment the principles that govern the irrigation of the tract of country lying between the Ganges and Jumna. This tract is known in Upper India as the Do-āb, or "two waters." It is the most instructive example of irrigation work in India. Made when comparatively little was known of canal engineering, every step taken in the construction of the Ganges Canal has been worked out from first principles ; every improvement has been made as the necessity has arisen. Thus it is not the mere arbitrary scheme of a single brain we are studying, but it must be remembered that the following considerations are the results of many years' experience of practical working, of numerous failures, and extensive remodelling. The opinions expressed are, in many cases, those gleaned in the course of professional work from some of the ablest irrigation officers in Northern India.

The necessity for undertaking irrigation works is usually forced upon the consideration of a government by the recurrence of disastrous droughts. It is suggested that these may be mitigated by the construction of irrigation works. An inquiry is instituted into the condition of the people, the suitability of the country to irrigation, and the source from which a sufficient supply of water may be obtained. Let us now follow the line of this inquiry.

The tract of country under consideration, the Do-āb, is a flat alluvial plain. It has been formed through the medium of the rivers Ganges and Jumna, from débris washed down from the Himalaya Mountains. Near the foot of the hills the soil contains boulders and stones brought down by mountain torrents. Leaving the mountains thirty miles or so, these disappear. Henceforth the soil is a fine river deposit. It varies much in character, from the lightest sand to the stiffest clay. These deposits are distributed in patches, sand and clay being found in juxtaposition, or one above the other. This formation is still going on, and forms a very interesting study which we may just touch on here.

The chief characteristic of an Indian river is the marvellous difference between its dry weather volume and that which it discharges in flood. This is due to the variability of the rainfall. Thus every Indian river possesses a broad valley, capable of taking the heavy floods. Within this valley is a small tortuous channel that contains the river during the greater part of the year. The main valley is well below the country, and does not change to any great extent. The dry weather channel is constantly cutting its way in the soft soil from one side of the valley to the other. A single heavy flood will often obliterate last year's channel, and form an entirely new one.

The following is an example of how the very patchy formation of the Do-āb has come about. A heavy flood is pouring down a valley. Its velocity is very great, for the current no longer follows the tortuous windings of the inner channel, but flows straight from point to point, and the stream falls the same height in a much shorter distance. The flood is black or red with floating particles. The valley varies in width, and this body of water passes through a narrow gorge with great velocity. As it emerges into the wider valley beyond, its speed receives a check. Here it deposits all the coarser, heavier sand its current is no longer able to sweep along. The lighter finer particles go to form the clay. The slightest current keeps them moving, and they are only deposited in the still backwaters amongst the reeds and weeds. Apart from these direct river deposits, clay beds are forming at the bottoms of all swamps and depressions in the plains.

Thus the clay strata, though found everywhere throughout the Do-āb, are local and discontinuous. They play a most important part in checking the flow of subsoil drainage. They form the great essential feature in the system of well irrigation that has been carried out from time immemorial. Imagine a stratum of clay some few hundred yards in extent, surrounded on all sides, and above and below by water-bearing sand. If a hole be pierced through this stratum, no alteration of the régime will occur. But let a masonry well be sunk down to the stratum and the hole pierced beneath the well. If we empty the well from above water will rush in from beneath the clay. Were the well merely sunk the same depth into water-bearing sand (putting aside all question of foundation) it would soon exhaust the water immediately around; its place would only be taken very slowly by water trickling in from a distance, not driven thither by any force or head. The clay stratum provides the well with a large collecting area. The head outside, which is not perceptibly diminished, drives in the water with a certain amount of energy towards the well.

Throughout the Do-āb large patches of unculturable soil are to be found. These are due sometimes to a stratum of impermeable clay, lying so near the surface as to prevent the rain-water from descending. Very often they are caused by the presence of saline matter in the soil. The action of heat and water on these salts causes a white efflorescence to appear on the surface. This is known as "reh."

There remains still a most important feature. Numerous beds are found of a peculiar alluvial formation of limestone. This generally is found in the form of nodular lumps, but sometimes in strata 1 ft. to 2 ft. in thickness. These beds are local and generally small in extent. They play a most-important part in the economy of the Do-āb, for this "kunker," as the stone is called, makes a good and often hydraulic lime. Its presence has added greatly to the facilities of engineering in Upper India.

We are now in a position to picture to ourselves this great plain of arable land, with its soil varying from the most highly productive to that of the poorest description. Here and there the dead level is relieved by rising ground where the light soil has been blown into low hills. Patches of barren land are met with here and there. These sometimes afford good grazing for the cattle; at others they present to the eye a surface glaring white, with salty efflorescence, like a field of snow. On the confines of the plain we descend into the great river valley through a network of ravines. These have been stripped by the heavy rains of almost every vestige of vegetable mould. In places they are absolutely bare; in others they are clothed with scrub and coarse spear grass, a paradise of hares and partridges, and the retreat of the wild boar.

Over all the plain, at intervals of a mile or two, are dotted the native villages. Some are merely a collection of a few mud hovels; others are larger, with more pretentious brick dwellings, and handsome temples. But, except in respect of size, each village is the counterpart of the others. The houses are built of mud, with flat roofs, and are huddled close together. The walls are irregular, and leaning inwards. There are no isolated dwellings on the Indian plains. Fear of attack in past days drove the villagers to herd together for mutual protection. It has become a custom, and the Indians are the slaves of custom. Every village has its pond or tank from which the mud had gone to make the houses. The older the village the larger the tank, and the village site has become a conical hill, for year after year the mud dwellings collapse, and new ones are built upon their ruins. Close by the village is a grove of mango trees, and one or two great banyan trees shelter an altar, and form a pleasant meeting place for village gossips. Far from the villages the trees are few and far between. Beneath their shade crops will not flourish. The trees mean luxuries, fruit and firewood; the crops mean life. There are no hedges nor ditches between the fields, nor hedge along the roadside. When the cattle go out to graze, a small boy with a stick serves well to fence them in. The villagers are not inclined to trespass on each other's land, and one field is known from another by the narrow strip of no man's land left unploughed in between.

The inhabitants of these mud villages are as various in race and creed as the soils of their own plain. They have been deposited by human inundations. Though they are all similarly employed in agricultural pursuits and bound together by the closest ties of mutual self-interest, still Rajput and low-cast Hindu, Mahomedan and gipsy, all preserve their race distinctions with the most jealous care. Not only do the various races preserve their individuality, each family also preserves its own social position. The leather-worker's son is a leather-worker, the shepherd's son a shepherd. The result is an utter absence of ambition, astonishing to the western mind, and a placid contentment that the bustling European often envies. This population depends entirely on agriculture for its existence. It is so dense that the soil only produces sufficient for the bare necessities of life. A cloth for the waist, a turban for the head, and a meal of baked flour and water once a day. They have no iron, no coal, no forests. They have no manufactures beyond the simple village trades. These do not soar above making a pair of shoes or a rough plough. Of course, here, as in every country, there are a few workers in wood or metals who almost attain the rank of artists. They are hereditary artists—not heaven-born. They evolve nothing new. They merely do skilfully what their ancestors have done before them. With the exception of these few necessary artisans, the whole of the population, when there is work to be done, labours in the fields. When there is no work, it sits in the sun, smokes, and enjoys the pleasures of a limited conversation. An absorbing topic of conversation is usually supplied by the smaller copper coins of the realm. Few can read. No books or papers penetrate to these far-off spots, and the people are supremely indifferent to all that goes on beyond the boundaries of their villages. Such is the life led by millions. They take no interest in the agitators who profess to represent them, and they know nothing of their politics.

NECESSITY OF IRRIGATION.

It is now obvious that the production of good crops, and more especially good food crops, is the one essential necessary to the welfare of this simple people. We should therefore examine the various climatic and other influences that bear upon the subject. We must endeavour to find if by any means we can neutralise the evil and strengthen the good.

The two essentials to the growth of crops are heat and moisture. The first of these, heat, we have, in a varying degree it is true, yet sufficient throughout the whole year for the growth of some or other crop. In the winter months the heat is great enough to grow wheat and barley, the ordinary English vegetables, and opium. In the summer months it is intense, and rice, millets, indigo, and sugar are the staple crops.

Thus as regards heat, the Do-āb leaves nothing to be desired. Any attempt to improve on it would merely result in the discomfiture of the inhabitants.

With regard to moisture the case is different. Except during the rainy months the country is decidedly arid. The rains last from the middle of June to the end of September, and are generally very heavy. It is not a very uncommon occurrence for more than 10 in. to fall in a single day. About Christmas there are usually a few wet days. The main crop of cereals is sown in October and reaped in March. The ground is prepared months before the sowings by occasional ploughing. Sugar is sown early in the spring and reaped after Christmas. Indigo is sown later and cut in the rains. Rice is sometimes sown early with irrigation, sometimes it is entirely a rain crop. The tall millets are grown in the rains and reaped in the autumn.

If the summer rains are plentiful there is sufficient moisture in the ground to make the wheat and barley germinate ; and if the winter rains are also good, the result will be an excellent crop. But these crops are always heavier when the rainfall is supplemented by irrigation. Sugar and indigo, opium and vegetables cannot be grown without the aid of irrigation. Thus we see that most crops are improved by artificial irrigation, and that for many it is an absolute necessity.

What then are the resources that the villagers have at their disposal for watering their lands? They dam up the smaller streams, and lead the water in earthen channels on to the adjacent fields. They lift the water from the tanks and swamps in which the rainfall has collected. But by far the most important source from which they draw their water supply is from their wells.

These wells vary in depth from a few feet to 30 or 40 yards. They are of four distinct kinds :—

1. Masonry wells, either of brick or of block kunkur, sunk down to a bed of clay. A hole a few inches in diameter is then jumped through the clay, and taps the water-bearing stratum beneath.

FIG. 1.

2. Simple wells with no lining, but dug throughout in stiff clay until water is reached. These are practically as good as masonary wells.

3. Simple wells in light soil tapping water below the clay in the same manner. These are liable to fall in when the ground becomes saturated from heavy rainfall.

4. Shallow wells in light soil for collecting the surface drainage. These generally fall in after working for some time.

The two first of these are termed stable wells, the two latter unstable. The shallow wells are worked by hand with the assistance of a contrivance called a "dhenkli." This consists of a pole about 15 ft. long, pivotted about 4 ft. from the thick end, which is counterweighted. About 10 ft. from the edge of the well a forked branch of a tree is let into the ground, the fork standing up about 4 ft. In this fork the pivot is fixed so as to allow the pole to swing vertically. To the long end of the pole, which comes directly over the mouth of the well, an earthen pot is attached by a cord of suitable length. (Fig. 1.) This simple contrivance with its counter-weight greatly facilitates the lifting of water from wells not more than 10 ft. or 15 ft. deep.

For greater depths than this there are several methods employed, but by far the most common is the direct pull of a pair of bullocks. About 6 ft. above the mouth of the well is fixed a large wooden pulley. The rope passes over this and is harnessed to the bullocks, who walk away from the well, and so lift the bucket, which is a large one made of leather, 3 ft. or 4 ft. in diameter. To assist the bullocks and take up less space, a ramp or bullock run is constructed up to the edge of the well; part of this is raised and part excavated. Thus the bullocks, when drawing water, are always walking down hill. (Fig. 2.)

Every locality is not, however, suitable to the construction of wells. Clay beds are not always available. The sand is too light to admit of the construction of simple wells. Masonry wells are expensive. The depth of the subsoil water and the cost of working are prohibitive. Sometimes the water is brackish, and unsuitable for irrigation purposes. Still, on the whole, the number of wells in the province was very great indeed, and when things went well the inhabitants were not to be pitied. But, alas! things very often turn out wrong, and we must consider the case of the villagers when they have to contend with unfavourable seasons.

The principal cause of distress is the erratic behaviour of the rainfall. At times it will be so heavy as to swamp the rice fields, strip the millets, and rot the sugar cane. The soil becomes waterlogged, and the unstable wells collapse and are thrown out of gear for the ensuing winter.

FIG. 2.

But a more serious cause of distress is the failure of the rainfall. The streams dry up. All moisture is drawn from the soil, and now the villagers turn to their wells, and they serve them in right good stead. The drought continues and the spring level sinks lower and lower. At last it recedes below the well curbs altogether. The wells are dry and famine stares the people in the face. There is nothing in the wide world that they can do to save themselves. The cattle and the crops die of thirst. The villagers seek the banks of their sacred snow-fed rivers, the Ganges and the Jumna, there to assuage their thirst and perish of starvation. We can realise the scene and we can well imagine how without a helping hand from Government, the country would be left a depopulated waste.

It was mainly to prevent the recurrence of such famines that the Ganges Canal, 400 miles in length, and with innumerable branches, was designed and commenced some forty years ago by Sir Proby Cantley. Its development is still in progress.

The canal has achieved a brilliant success, but many slight inconveniences have arisen that have had to be overcome, and which, could they have been foreseen, would have saved much trouble and expense. Hence, in projecting a scheme of this kind, it is necessary to anticipate, and as far as possible to devise means to modify all contingencies that may arise to neutralise its beneficial effects.

We will therefore now enumerate some of the objections which may be urged against canal irrigation, and which should be exhaustively discussed before deciding to introduce it into any particular district.

First arises the question, "Are irrigation works necessary?" Might not the fear of absolute famine be put aside by the opening up the country by railways, so that grain may be poured into any district at a moment's notice. Where would the grain be stored for such purposes? What would be the loss of interest in thus hoarding it away, what loss by deterioration? Would it be practicable were the famine universal and not merely local?

Again, the interference of the Government may render the villagers discontented, make them lazy, and take away their self-reliance. They will perhaps abandon drawing water from their wells altogether, and prefer the less laborious occupation of watching canal water flow over their fields. The cattle will deteriorate, since they are no longer required to raise the water. The facilities for production will lead to over-cropping and gradually impoverish the soil. Lands near the canal will become water-logged. The general spring level of the country will be raised by percolation and malarious fevers will increase ; and lastly, when their wells are abandoned, their cattle gone, and the cultivator become enervated and effeminate, in the midst of an exceptionally dry season, some accident will happen to throw the whole canal out of gear for several years.

The answer to all these objections is the same. Your scheme must be designed and carried out intelligently.

The cultivator must not be harassed or interfered with unnecessarily. The existing wells must not be interfered with, canal water only introduced into tracts where there are no wells, or only unstable ones. Over-cropping must be discouraged by only permitting a limited supply of water. Percolation must be prevented by clay puddling, and the superfluous water introduced by the canal provided for by suitable drainage schemes.

Accident must be guarded against by every human precaution, and by making every member of the establishment responsible for the portion of which he holds charge.

SOURCE OF WATER SUPPLY.

Having arrived at the conclusion that an extensive system of irrigation is necessary for the proper development of the agriculture of the province, and that the advantages to be derived will outweigh the disadvantages, a suitable project must be worked out, and firstly its feasibility, and secondly its financial soundness, thoroughly tested. The character of the scheme that can be adopted will vary according to the source of water supply available. Generally speaking these sources are of five kinds, and each of these in turn has been utilised in the development of some or other tract of country in India. The five kinds of irrigation scheme derived from these sources are briefly as follows :

1. An extensive system of deep masonry wells, tapping an almost permanent supply of water. This system is suitable to small isolated communities, which have not sufficient capital or resources to undertake more comprehensive schemes, or whose geographical position may render the introduction of lines of canal difficult. The area commanded by these wells is limited, and they can only be constructed in particular places where the soil, &c., is suitable. This is perhaps the most ancient form of irrigation scheme in Northern India; it has been recently revived on a large scale by the Department of Agriculture and Commerce. It has

been employed with satisfactory results in the development of certain native states administered, during the minority of their rulers, by the Government Court of Wards. The supply from this source is perennial.

2. The tank system has been largely employed in Southern India. It is more suitable to a hilly or undulating country, and consists in placing dams or "bunds" across depressions or valleys, and collecting the rain water for use during the ensuing dry season.

3. Canals which derive their supply from a river, which, owing to the absence of snow from its collecting grounds, has no permanent high supply. A high dam is constructed across some suitable gorge in the river bed, and the wide valley behind turned into a lake. When the river ceases to give a sufficient supply, the reserve in this lake is drawn

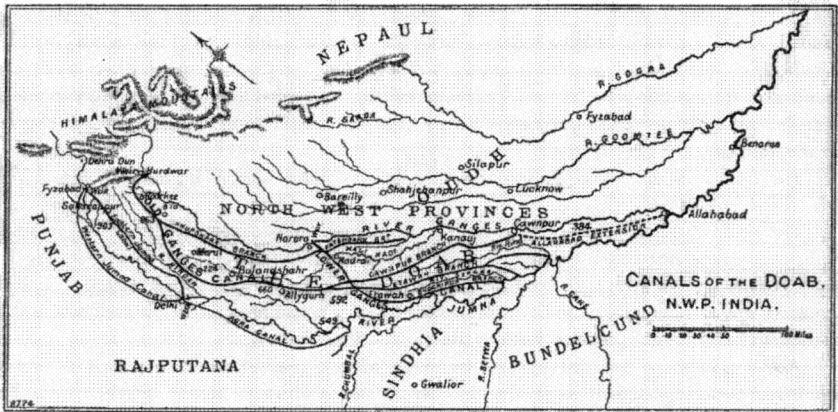

Fig. 3.

upon. Water from this source is usually only available during the autumn and winter months. It is an insurance, however, against famine The excellency of this system of irrigation is based on the principle that half a loaf is better than no bread. A good example of this kind of canal has recently been completed in Bundelcund, where others of a similar nature have been projected.

4. Inundation canals fed from the flood waters of rivers whose banks are higher than the general country. These are only available for irrigation during the months in which the river remains in flood, whether caused by the melting of snow or to rainfall in the collecting grounds. Large rivers supplied from distant mountains are often in heavy flood during the driest seasons of the plains they traverse.

5. Perennial canals, drawing their supply from snow-fed rivers. These vary in volume, it is true, but never fall below a certain minimum supply. These canals are found in Northern India, tapping the great rivers that have their sources amongst the glaciers of the Himalayas, and drawing their high summer supplies from the melting of the extensive snowfields lying just below the line of perpetual snow.

It is this last system of irrigation alone that it is proposed to describe, for although the sources of supply and the methods of obtaining water are so varied, still the general principles of water distribution and supervision are the same in all cases.

In the present article will be briefly stated the main considerations that require earnest attention before proceeding to elaborate a scheme. The first consideration is whether the general slope of the country admits of water from the river being carried over the greater part of its surface. Secondly, the best method of conveying the water from the river and distributing it over the country at the least possible cost, and with the least possible waste of water. The general lie of the country will decide from which of the two rivers bounding the tract our supply is to be drawn, or whether it will not be advisable to utilise both; and in studying this aspect of the case, the lie of the districts beyond the rivers, and their suitability for irrigation, must not be selfishly excluded. In the example we have chosen, it would be obviously impossible to irrigate the country lying to the west of the River Hindan from the Ganges Canal, the levels being adverse to such a project. This portion must, therefore, depend on the Jumna for its supply of canal water. It is irrigated by the Eastern Jumna Canal. (Fig. 3.)

The river having been decided on, a dam will be thrown across it at some suitable spot, so as to insure a constant supply and head up the water as much as possible, without disturbing the régime of the river. The main line of canal will be taken by the shortest or easiest route to the main watershed of the country. It will follow this watershed as far as possible. Branches will be taken down the secondary or the terminal watersheds of the tracts. From these branches distributaries and minor distributaries will carry the water along the spurs that lie between the smaller streams or ravines. Thus, since a canal is meant to pour water on to a country, whilst the function of a river is to drain it off, a well-constructed canal should in every respect be exactly the reverse of the river. It will flow on the highest instead of in the lowest ground. Instead of being reinforced by tributaries and gathering water as it flows on, it is constantly being reduced in volume by its branches, and these, again, by the distributaries and minor distributaries. It will eventually terminate by pouring out water in every direction, on those very fields that form the source or collecting grounds of the river. The rivers carry their greatest volume in the wettest seasons, the canals should then be dry, and should carry their highest supply in times of drought.

ENGINEERING CONSIDERATIONS.

It is often impossible to take the canal on to the watershed of the country without crossing a number of mountain torrents or tributaries.

The determination of the best and most permanent, and at the same time economical methods of crossing these, will cause much anxiety and careful thought. This is perhaps one of the biggest subjects in canal engineering, including, as it sometimes does, the protection of the canal from obliteration by the wash down from the adjacent hills.

There are many other difficulties that will have to be faced by the projector. The watershed may become so tortuous as to render it advisable to abandon its line at places and take a more direct route. Low necks of land or extensive swamps may be encountered, necessitating heavy embankments, or there may be met with hills or ridges requiring very deep cutting.

The soil will often be found so rotten that it is scarcely capable of holding water, or so sandy that the banks may be constantly slipping away.

An important question is that of labour. The engineer may perhaps be able to obtain the amount of unskilled labour he requires for simple earthwork, but he will require as well skilled masons, carpenters, engine-drivers, smiths, divers, and men capable of supervising them. This labour question was a very serious one when the Jumna and Ganges Canals were started. The officers had then to drill their workmen and teach them the elements almost of their trades. Now there is always a very fair number of skilled workmen available for any large work. These men generally have their own small properties, which, during their absence, are worked by their sons or brothers. When they are thrown out of work they return to agriculture and their own homes, from which they may be collected on the shortest notice. Different classes seem to take naturally to the different branches of engineering. The best people for doing large pieces of earthwork are the Purbeahs from the eastern provinces, who go about in gangs, setting up simple villages of grass huts wherever their work calls them. The men dig, the women and children carry basket-loads of earth, whilst the smaller babies lie in the sun. The bricklayers and stonemasons are local men from the different villages of the North-West Provinces, mostly Mahomedans. The best fitters and carpenters are from the Punjab. These men are strong and reliable, with a happy disposition and a strong sense of humour, very different from the Hindoos of the more easterly districts. As divers and for employment in sloppy work they are unrivalled. The Khallassies from Bombay are unequalled for work up aloft, and making scaffolding.

The question of materials for the construction of our masonry works is an absorbing one. Are there stone quarries available, or is the land suitable for the manufacture of sufficiently good bricks? Can we obtain good lime in the neighbourhood of our projected works, and how? Where will the fuel for our brick and lime manufacture come from? Will it be wood or coal? Can we obtain the wood necessary for our piles, centerings, or scaffolding, and whence? The means of transport for these materials and the time that they will take to collect must be carefully looked into. All these and many other points must be well weighed and long pondered over in order that we may arrive at a tolerably correct estimate of our future expense, and thus enable us to face the financial aspect of the question with some degree of confidence, and to prevent all fear of utter financial failure.

FINANCIAL CONSIDERATIONS.

Taking into consideration the varying kinds of soil which our canal is designed to irrigate, and the prevailing crops (and remembering that with the introduction of canal water, the character of these crops will undergo a change and new varieties be introduced), we must calculate what area can be irrigated by the water available from our source of supply. This source of supply is itself variable. The highest floods occur during the rains. When these cease the river gradually falls till it reaches its minimum in March or April. With the hot weather the melting of the lower snows commences, and thanks to these a good supply is maintained until the breaking of the rainy season. Should, however, the arrival of the rainy season be very long deferred indeed, the available snowfields may melt away, and the rivers will depend entirely on the supply of water always given by the great glaciers. In this case the river may fall considerably in July or August when rain or fresh snow is certain to fall in the mountains. It has been determined roughly by numerous discharge measurements, that the average volume of the Ganges obtainable for the winter crops of cereals is about two-thirds of that available when snow water comes down for irrigating the summer crops of sugar and indigo.

Thus assuming the winter volume in the river at the head of our canal to be 4000 cubic feet per second, the volume available in the summer months will be about 6000 cubic feet per second. The canal should be designed to carry this latter volume, as it is most important to be able to supply the country with as much water as possible during the hot season.

The area that can be irrigated in a season by one cubic foot per second running constantly is termed the "duty" of the water. It is an exceedingly variable factor. The main causes of fluctuation in the duty of canal water are : 1. Variation of temperature, the duty being much higher in cold than in hot weather. 2. Condition of the soil, whether partially saturated or quite dry. 3. Character of the soil. Sandy soil giving a much lesser duty than clay owing to its absorptive qualities. 4. Care with which the land is irrigated.

It will be seen that our premises are so very variable as to put mathematical calculations out of the question. It has, however, been found from experience that certain averages always hold good. The duty of water can only be determined by experiment, and experiments for this end have been most carefully conducted both with canal and well water, and for various kinds of soil. An average has been struck and is now used as a basis of calculation in preparing an irrigation project. The determination of duty by experiment is merely a matter of time and care. A carefully supervised staff of natives is kept for several seasons upon one tract of land. In the case of wells every bucket of water that comes up is counted ; in the case of canal water the discharge of the outlets and the length of time they run each day are carefully recorded. At the end of each season the area of land irrigated is noted and the duty deduced. The books kept by men employed in such experiments should contain as much collateral information as possible. The number of waterings given to each field, the manner in which they have been given, the intervals between them, the amount of rain fallen, and the result—whether the crop is good, bad, or indifferent. At the same time remarks should be inserted by the experimenter as to any causes to which he or the cultivator may attribute an exceptionally good or exceptionally bad outturn. The experiments should prove a valuable guide for the future use of agricultural engineers.

Supposing that as a result of our experiments we find that on the average one cubic foot of water per second is sufficient to irrigate 90 acres during the hot and 180 acres during the cold season, we can now calculate the area that our canal should command.

The average available volume during the hot season is 6000 cubic feet per second, the duty of each cubic foot is 90 acres. Hence the area commanded will be 6000 × 90 = 54,000 acres. The volume during the cold season is 4000 cubic feet, the duty is 180 acres. Hence the area commanded in the cold season will be 4,000 × 180 = 720,000 acres. From these a deduction for loss by percolation and evaporation during the long journey from the river must be made. Allowing 10 per cent. for these losses, the area we can command is about 500,000 acres in the hot season, and 640,000 acres in the cold season. Taking the cold weather supply as our basis of calculation, arrangements may be made for the irrigation of 640,000 acres, equal to 1000 square miles. This area is, however, not one-twentieth part of the whole area of the Do-âb. We must therefore consider in what proportions the supply is to be distributed so as to avoid injustice and unnecessary expense, and also whether it will not be possible to reinforce the canal supply from any other source.

If a dam be placed across an Indian river and every drop of water in the river diverted into the canal, the river immediately below will be quite dry. We have, however, only to proceed a few miles down the river bed to find it a flowing stream again, and 100 miles or so further on it will contain a very considerable volume. This accession of water is due partly to percolation in the river bed below the dam, partly to the subsoil drainage from the high lands, and partly to tributaries that flow in in the interval. We can, therefore, if necessary, reinforce our canal from lower down the river by constructing a dam and head similar to those above.

Now with regard to the fair distribution of the water thus obtained, we may assume as a preliminary basis that it is unnecessary to supply with canal water lands coming under the following heads. Such lands may therefore be eliminated from our calculations :

1. Unculturable waste lands.
2. Low-lying lands that remain constantly moist.
3. Lands already supplied with water from other sources, such as wells or tanks.
4. And possibly bad sandy tracts which absorb an immense amount of water without an adequate return in the way of increased fertility.

If statistics concerning the area of land coming under these various heads are not available, as much information as possible must be acquired during the preliminary surveys ; and later on the officers in charge of the construction of branches and distributaries be warned against introducing water into lands classed as above.

In every village in the North-West Provinces a most careful record is kept of the ownership of the land and its classification. Each field is numbered, and the numbers are written on a large scale map of the village showing every field. One copy of this map is kept in the village and another at the head-quarters of the district. A book descriptive of the fields is also kept up. This book contains all details concerning the fields, their area, a description of the soil, the names of owner and of occupier, and whether the fields are irrigated or not. When, therefore, it is proposed to introduce canal irrigation into a district the civil authorities are first requested to supply all necessary statistics in the following form or in one of a similar nature.

SCHEDULE OF AREA.

Name of District.	Name of Village.	Total Area.	Culturable Area.									Unculturable Waste.	Remarks.
			Unirrigated.					Irrigated from Wells and Tanks.					
			Light Sandy Soil.	Fairly Good Soil.	Rich Manured	Waste.	Total.	Light Sandy Soil.	Fairly Good Soil.	Rich Manured.	Total.		
1	2	3	4	5	6	7	8	9	10	11	12	13	14

The sum of columns 4 to 7 will represent the total area requiring irrigation, but if the sandy soil is found from inspection not to be sufficiently productive to justify an expenditure of water upon it, column 4 may be eliminated.

It has been assumed above that the main canal will supply sufficient water to irrigate 640,000 acres, and that it can be reinforced from a point lower down the river by, say, half as much again. It will now be capable of irrigating during the cold weather months 640,000 + 320,000 = 960,000 acres of land, equal to 1500 square miles. If the total dry culturable area of the province be not out of all proportion to this, say not more than ten times as great, an effort should be made to divide the water as far as practicable amongst the villages proportionally to the dry culturable area of each. But if the proportion be much greater, part of the province must be omitted from the scheme, as the expense of making and maintaining very long channels to do a comparatively small amount of irrigation will be prohibitive. The portions of the province selected to be brought under irrigation should have an aggregate dry culturable area of about 15,000 square miles. They will be chosen, firstly, for their proximity to the sources of supply, and, secondly, with regard to the general character of their soil.

In the Do-áb the supply from both the Ganges and Jumna canals is sufficient to provide almost the whole culturable area with a fair proportion of water. The north-west tract commanded by the Jumna Canal is of course left out of the Ganges Canal calculations and vice versâ. The part of the Do-áb, south of Cawnpore, was originally omitted from the scheme, but owing to improvements in water regulation and greater economy, this portion is now also to be brought under canal irrigation.

Now suppose that certain tracts, whose dry culturable areas aggregate about 15,000 square miles, have been fixed upon as suitable for our purpose, during the cold weather, one-tenth part of the dry culturable area of each village can be irrigated, and nearly as much again during the hot season. It has been mentioned above that double-cropping is injurious to the fields, and should be discouraged This watering, therefore, of one-tenth of the dry area twice a year should be equivalent to watering one-fifth of the dry cultivated area during the year. When it is remembered that, say, one-seventh of the land should lie fallow every year, and that some of the culturable waste that has been included in our estimate will probably be kept unwatered as grazing ground for cattle, the proportion irrigated will rise to nearly one-third of the dry cultivated area in each village. This proportion will in many instances rise much higher; for many villages, whose soil is poor or land high lying will not take to irrigation as a general practice. It will be seen from the above considerations that the canal projector is liable to fall into the error of providing water in too great abundance, rather than in too small proportion. Water, when applied to irrigation purposes, is wonderfully elastic. This is very patent to any one who compares the care with which the cultivator doles out each bucketful from his well, and the reckless way in which he turns canal water over his carelessly prepared fields.

DRAINAGE.

We have seen that the main subjects to be considered by the projector of an irrigation scheme are the following :

1. The general slope of the country.
2. The reliable supply of water available.
3. The area to be brought under irrigation and its location.
4. The general arrangement of the canal and its branches.
5. The engineering difficulties to be contended with.

There are several side issues that must not be neglected if he wishes his scheme to be perfect from the commencement, and he must add to the above :

6. The question of percolation, water logging, and drainage.
7. Escape power, necessary for the regulation and safety of the canal.
8. Plantations and reclamation of land.
9. Navigation whether to be provided for or not.

Experience has shown the question of drainage, or the rapid removal of superfluous water, to be of the most vital importance to the success of a canal scheme. Only a very small percentage of canal water is legitimately utilised by actual absorption into the crops themselves, the remainder is disposed of by evaporation or percolation, or runs off into the rivers through the natural drainage channels of the country.

Evaporation has probably a beneficial effect on the economy of a country, which suffers, during a greater part of the year, from the dryness of its atmosphere. The water which percolates through the soil goes to raise the spring level of the subsoil water ; and it has been shown by experience that this spring level cannot be raised beyond certain limits without producing deleterious effects upon the health of the district. The amount carried off by natural drainage channels is comparatively slight during the dry seasons of the year, as the running to waste of any considerable volume of canal water is such an evident sign of bad management or waste, that it would not long be permitted to continue unchecked. But there are times when the disposal of this water becomes a matter of very serious importance. Take the case of sudden rainfall occurring when canal irrigation is in full swing. The cultivators, fearful of swamping their fields, block up the irrigating channels, and the water, thus hindered from flowing over the fields, finds its outlet through the natural drainage channels. These, owing to the sudden rainfall, are probably already bank full. The result will be overflowing and damage to adjoining fields and villages.

The questions of percolation and drainage are so intimately connected with the provision of proper escape power for the canal system that they will be considered together. Percolation from the irrigated fields themselves, if the irrigation is properly conducted, is not a very great source of danger, it is comparatively small. It is intermittent and merely equivalent to an increased rainfall which the country can well stand. But the real danger is from direct percolation from the main canal and its branches. These have often a depth of 10 ft. or 12 ft., and pass through light sandy soil. When the canal passes through low-lying lands or through bad porous soil the country around will become water-logged, unless precautions are taken to mitigate the evil. These precautions may be either direct or indirect. The banks and bed of the canal may be rendered watertight, or a system of drainage must be devised to take off the superfluous water brought by the canal. It will be shown hereafter that the former condition may sometimes be partially attained by encouraging a deposit of fine clay on the banks and bed. This process, where practicable, will be very gradual. The rendering large canals water-tight by a clay or other lining is too costly a process almost to be considered. An extensive drainage scheme will therefore form a necessary portion of an irrigation project.

The study of this aspect of the question necessarily leads to an examination of the condition of the low-lying lands and swamps met with throughout the course of the canal. These will often be found to be imperfectly drained, often, indeed, to have no outfall at all. The people who live on the edges of these swamps relate how, in years of heavy rain, the waters rise above their wonted height and entirely destroy their crops of sugar, rice, or millets. They are unanimous in their opinion that, were these swamps drained, their condition would be materially improved. The agricultural engineer must not, however, draw hasty conclusions from the experience of one or two bad years and proceed, without further thought, to prepare drainage schemes for the whole country. He must look further ahead than the cultivator.

These swamps and blind drainages not only form tanks from which the villagers can draw a direct supply of water for their fields, but they are the reservoirs that keep the subsoil water at a proper level and maintain the supply of water for their wells. Were all the rain water to run off as quickly as it fell, the wells throughout the province would soon be rendered useless. The question of drainage of superfluous water is one that cannot be too strongly insisted on. In some cases the cheapest course to pursue may be to purchase outright the piece of land likely to suffer from swamping, and let it run to waste altogether. But you may rest assured that if you adopt this plan, one of your successors, less economically inclined, will undertake the reclamation of this land. It is needless to say that this reclamation, when the land is covered with a dense growth of coarse grass and jungle, will be a very expensive undertaking.

The distinguishing characteristic of an irrigation canal is its constantly diminishing volume. It is evident that where the main canal parts with water to its branches it will diminish in size, and will get smaller and smaller until it eventually becomes no more than a distributary itself. As long as there is a demand for water, and the branches are running, this causes no difficulty; but if on account of sudden rain, or some accident, it is found necessary to close one or more of the large branches, a volume of water, much greater than that for which they were designed, will be thrown upon the lower reaches. Unless provision is made for this contingency the results will be disastrous. For example, suppose the canal to be flowing with a velocity of two miles an hour, allowing only a few hours for the transmission of news to the head, it will take four days for a reduction of volume made at the head to be felt at the two-hundredth mile of the canal.

In order, therefore, to insure the safety of the canal, as well as to permit of greater delicacy of regulation, efficient escapes must be provided at intervals, down which superfluous water may be turned at a moment's notice. Carrying the same principle out more fully, we shall find that smaller escapes will be required upon all branches and distributaries. The location of these escape channels and the disposal of the water running through them becomes then a question of very great importance.

Where the canal is so situated as to admit of an escape channel being excavated direct to one of the principal rivers there is no question of the volume that can be discharged by it; but usually the canal is at such a distance from the river as to render this impossible. It then becomes necessary to utilise the smaller river channels, and in doing this the effects of introducing a large body of water into their valleys at all seasons of the year must be most carefully

B

studied. It must be remembered that although most of these streams carry a volume through the rains, beside which the quantity of escape water is comparatively insignificant ; yet, immediately the summer floods subside the valleys are ploughed up and sown throughout with wheat and barley.

The earlier the floods retire the greater the number of ploughings that can be given to the land, and a proportionately better crop is the result. Any cause, therefore, that may tend to prolong the period of flood is a distinct injury to the cultivators of these valleys.

Another way in which inconvenience may be caused by letting escape water into the dry weather channel of a small river is the interruption of traffic. The prevalent custom with such small streams is for the villagers to place dams across their beds after the rains, and to use what little water comes down for irrigation. They can cross the stream to their fields at almost any part. But with the introduction of an escape this system must necessarily be changed. The dams must be removed to admit of a free channel for the flow of escape water should it be found necessary to admit it, and instead of the simple fords, ferry boats or bridges will be required to convey the villagers across. The increased velocity of the stream may disturb the régime of the river, cause scour in the bed of the cold weather channel, and endanger the foundations of masonry works, such as road or railway bridges.

On the other hand, the introduction of waste canal water may greatly improve the dry weather channel of a river, by enlarging the channel and keeping it clear of weeds. This adds greatly to the stability of the channel, for the tendency to break away into new channels is always much greater when the old one becomes choked.

PLANTATIONS.

The question that next claims attention is the one of canal plantations. It has been customary in constructing canals in Northern India to plant a belt of trees on each side of the main canal and branches, and lines of shade trees along the distributaries and lesser channels

Fig. 4.

Fig. 5.

(see Fig. 4). Several objections have been urged against this practice ; first, on account of the damage done by the shade of large trees to the adjoining crops ; secondly, that the immense length, out of all proportion to the width, renders adequate protection either by fencing or by patrolling extremely expensive and difficult. It is contended that if plantations are required at all, square blocks, under the supervision of members of the Forest Department, will give much better results. Thirdly, that the canal plantations are irresistibly attractive to the village cattle, and constitute a continual source of friction between the villagers and the canal authorities. The shade lines along distributaries are also found to be injurious to the neighbouring cultivation. Against most of these objections arguments may be urged in favour of the retention of these plantations.

1. Where the shade of the trees is injurious to the adjacent fields, let the outside line of trees be kept so far within the boundary line that its shade will not appreciably reach beyond

2. The fact that the plantations are narrow strips running parallel to the canal renders their inspection by canal officials not only easy but unavoidable in the course of their ordinary work. Large square blocks of plantations would not afford the same facilities for the irrigation of young plants as do the strips running near the canal.

3. The village cattle will always find in the grassy slopes of the canal an irresistible temptation, whether there be plantations there or not.

4. The shady banks of the distributaries are much used by the villagers as footpaths, but the question has naturally arisen whether it is fair to confer benefits on the general public at the expense of the individuals whose crops are injured by the shade.

In the North-West Provinces these shade lines on distributaries have been abandoned, much to the discomfort of travellers and of the executive and assistant engineers who are obliged to ride along them in all seasons. The principal object in establishing canal plantations is to afford a supply of timber or firewood for use on the construction and maintenance of canal works, at the same time it is advisable to render the plantations self-supporting by selling timber and fuel in the nearest markets.

The projector has to consider at this stage of his project whether it is advisable to establish canal plantations or not, and whether they can be rendered self-supporting. Thus in stocking a plantation the subjects to be weighed are, what trees are best suited for the soil, for what class of wood will there be the greatest local demand, firewood or timber, what kind is most likely to be required for the canal works. Then, the distance from the nearest market, and the available means of transporting thither the produce of our plantations, lead naturally to a comparison of the cost of carriage by road, by rail, or by water, and the question arises whether the projected canal should be a navigable one or not ; what sacrifices will have to be made, what expenses incurred, and what returns from traffic may be expected.

NAVIGATION.

The main obstacles met with in making navigable canals in India are :

1. The difficulty of diverting the canal so as to pass close to large cities, and so tap important centres of trade.

2. The velocity of the current rendering the towing of boats up stream a slow and laborious process.

3. The growth of heavy jungle along the banks interfering with the tow ropes at certain seasons of the year. During the rains this jungle often attains a height of 15 ft. or 20 ft., and the keeping down of this growth involves very considerable expense.

4. The presence of numerous falls will involve the construction of locks.

5. The wash from steamers and launches plying on the canal may injure the banks.

The greater the slope of the country the greater will be the velocity of the current and the greater the number of falls.

Near the head of the Ganges Canal, where in the stony soil the current is very swift and the height and number of the falls is very great, it has been found advisable to make a separate lock channel altogether for several miles. Besides the locks and works necessary for getting traffic past the falls, all road and railway bridges over the canal must be made sufficiently high to admit of the boats passing underneath, or be provided with drawbridges or opening bays of some kind or another; for the principal traffic will be in native boats piled high with cotton or other light cargo. This will inconvenience the traffic over these bridges, and the question to be decided is whether it is worth the trouble and expense to make the canal navigable.

It must be remembered that the main canal runs along the backbone of the country, the portion where the fewest obstacles are to be encountered, and, therefore, the line naturally chosen as the highway of the province. This is conspicuously so in the North-West Provinces, the canals, high roads, and railways all running parallel and close alongside one another. First is made the high road, then comes the canal taking some traffic from the road, and, lastly, the railway steps in and supersedes to a great extent the canal and road as regards both goods and passenger traffic. Still, the great facilities that a navigable canal affords for the conveyance of heavy material to large isolated works, the great assistance rendered by boating to the development of the plantations and the advantages for inspection purposes, must not be overlooked. And if by means of direct and indirect returns the navigation can be made to pay it will seem advisable to adopt it.

If the engineer follows out the lines of thought indicated in the foregoing remarks it is believed that no contingency of any vital importance will be left unprovided for in his preliminary design and estimate. It is necessary for him now to look to the credit side of his account, to see from what sources his funds may be obtained, and whether the income derived from the works will justify the preliminary expenditure and the heavy annual cost of repairs and maintenance, with a considerable margin over for unforeseen contingencies such as would result from the failure of any important work. The sources of revenue will be mainly of two kinds.

REVENUE.

1. Direct revenue, or the payment for the use of canal water for irrigation purposes.

2. Indirect sources. The enhancement in the value of land due to the introduction of canal water.

Then there are receipts for the sale of canal water to municipalities or for building or other purposes, the sale of plantation products and of grass, and the returns from navigation traffic.

The first of these sources of revenue is the only one which at this early stage should be counted upon by the engineer. He should look on the indirect revenue as a sign of the general improvement of the country, allowing it to go to the amelioration of the condition of the people and the reduction of other taxes.

Later on the question of enhancement of rents and increase of land revenue due to introduction of irrigation may be discussed.

The receipts from plantations and navigation will be comparatively unimportant, and may be omitted at this stage.

Water used for the purposes of irrigation may be charged for in three different ways :

1. By the quantity available for use by the cultivator, whether he uses that amount or not. The adoption of this system requires that an unvarying supply of water shall always be available for his use, and implies the adoption of some form of outlet that will always give a constant discharge, and which will be unaffected by variations in the supply of water in the canal.

2. By the actual quantity of water taken by the cultivators. This implies the use of some form of water meter, absolutely accurate, and which cannot be tampered with.

3. By the area of land irrigated during a season. This requires no mechanical arrange- ment for its measurement, but the maintenance of a considerable staff to note what fields have been irrigated, and make measurements of the areas watered. The latter is the system that has been adopted in the irrigation of the Do-āb; it gives no absolute account of the actual quantity of water used, for the amount of water used to irrigate equal areas is not necessarily the same. This variability in the quantity of water required to irrigate equal areas is in many cases explicable. One cause lies in the constitution of the soil. A light sandy soil will swallow up a much greater quantity of water than a stiff heavy soil. Another cause is the varying amount of water required for the various kinds of crops, and the condition of the soil (whether wet or dry) when the watering is given. It is found, however, that similar crops are to a great extent grown on similar soils, so that the presence of a particular crop will demonstrate the presence of a particular soil ; it is, therefore, unnecessary, since our calculations, at the best, can only be of an approximate nature, to consider the two causes separately, but take the variation of crops as representative of both. A fair way, therefore, of levying water rate will be to charge so much per acre for a given class of crop. The actual amount of water used per acre will vary from field to field, but over a large extent the average quantity will be nearly constant.

In the Do-āb the numerous crops have been divided into four classes, according to the quantity of water they require. The first class contains crops such as rice and sugar-cane, requiring a large quantity of water for their growth, and so on downwards, the fourth class containing poor crops that require very little water. The amount that can be charged per acre for canal water can only be arrived at after careful experiments and consultation with the most experienced men of the district. And great care must be taken in the fixing of this water rate, as once fixed it will be found very difficult to enhance it.

The experiments should take the line indicated below. The products of a field of unirri- gated and one of irrigated grain grown near together at the same time must be compared. The difference between their values will be the maximum amount that might be exacted as water rate. The average of numbers of experiments of this kind carried out through several seasons will give the required result. There are, however, some crops that are never grown without irrigation, and in this case the cost of raising water from the wells may be taken as a maximum water rate. The fact must not be lost sight of, however, that generally the bullocks employed in this work are necessary to the cultivator for tilling his land, and that were they not employed in lifting water, they might be standing idle. In a country like India, where irrigation has been resorted to for centuries, the cost of irrigating an acre of land in different localities is generally well known to the cultivators.

It has been assumed, so far, that the canal water is poured direct upon the field, but such is not always the case. It is often impossible to command a tract of country so that the water will flow over it. In this case the villagers have to lift the water up to the level of their fields. Sometimes this height is only a few inches, at others it is as much as 6 ft. or 7 ft. The method usually adopted for raising water in the North-West Provinces is shown in the sketches Figs. 6 and 7. A basket, generally lined with leather to render it watertight, is suspended by

Fig. 6.

Fig. 7.

four strings; with this a couple of men bale up the water. They acquire great skill in working these lifts. The action is much that of rowing, and they fling the water up rather than lift it. Some grass or a grass mat serves to protect the earth from the wash.

Since the cultivator has now to employ labour, the value of the water has for him decreased, and his water rate must be reduced. The height lifted should regulate this reduction, but in practice, owing to irregularities in the ground and variability in the height of the canal water, the heights lifted are too variable to admit of nice distinctions. In the Do-āb the charge for "lift" irrigation has been arbitrarily fixed at one-half of that for "flow" irrigation of a similar crop. This great difference will not astonish us so much when we remember that the cultivators are much more careful of lift than of flow water.

CANAL AND DISTRIBUTARY ALIGNMENT.

It has been already stated that the main line of the canal follows the principal watershed of the country. The reason for this is plain. As the object of the canal is to irrigate the country, the main supply channel should be situated on the highest ground (Fig. 8), as this is the only position that can give a complete command of the whole surface

Were the canal aligned off the main watershed we should have the condition of things shown in Fig. 9. Very high embankment would have to be resorted to in order to command the highest ground, unless this high-lying land be abandoned, or only irrigated by the laborious process of lifting water. Such alignment will evidently interfere with drainage and lead to the swamping of the land between the canal and the watershed. The same arguments apply to the secondary or distributing channels.

Although this principle was clearly recognised in the design for the main line of the Ganges Canal, it appears to have been overlooked in the construction of the distributing channels. It was very rightly assumed to be a general principle that no irrigation should be done directly from the main line of canal or principal branches, as the cost of making numerous outlets in the great banks would be large, and these outlets would, in high banks, be a fruitful source of anxiety. In order to effect the distribution of water with as little danger to the main canal as possible, Sir Proby Cautley designed two main distributing channels running parallel to and at a short distance from the canal. In order to prevent these channels from assuming too large proportions, and so rendering them liable to the same objections as were urged against the main canal as a distributing agent, their channels were only designed to carry sufficient water for the supply of a few square miles of country. Their supply had, therefore, to be reinforced at intervals of two or three miles through feeders from the main canal. The main distributaries were also provided with escapes at intervals. The result of this system, carried out fully, is a gridiron arrangement of water channels like that shown in Fig. 10, or a modification like that shown in Fig. 11. The designer, in a circular addressed to his executive officers, particularly impressed upon them that the alignments of the main distributaries and feeders must be made with care and intelligence, that straightness and regularity must give way to the exigencies of the ground. The system, however, was incompatible with the watershed alignment mentioned, and it was found that most of the drainage of the country was intercepted and collected in the pockets A A, where it swamped the fields and breached the distributary banks. When this system was found to work unsatisfactorily, it was determined to break the continuity of the right and left main distributaries so as to offer less obstruction to the flow of drainage water. Extensive remodelling schemes were therefore undertaken on the lines indicated in Fig. 12. The main distributaries were broken up into a series of independent channels.

The result of this remodelling was not altogether satisfactory, the distributaries still crossed depressions in many places and passed through a great deal of barren land. Meantime other canals were being constructed in the North-West Provinces outside the Do-áb, and in order to avoid repeating the mistakes that had been made in the Ganges Canal branches, some of their distributaries were aligned as shown in Fig. 13. These channels were not designed to make certain fixed angles with the canal, but intelligently laid out with due regard to the nature of the country. They were, however, ranged out in perfectly straight lines. There is a simplicity about this arrangement that recommends itself to the engineer were it compatible with efficiency in other ways.

In the alignment of distributing channels we should keep the following obvious principles in mind :

1. To keep the water on the highest ground.

24

Fig. 8.

Fig. 9.

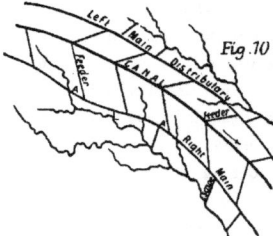

Fig. 10

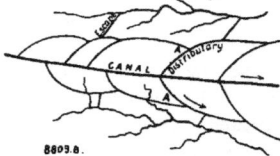

Fig. 11.

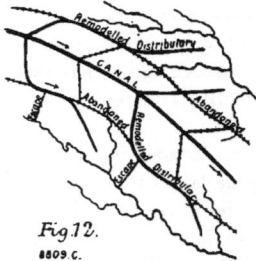

Fig. 12.

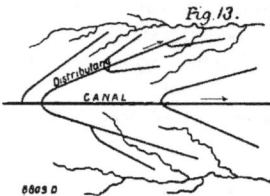

Fig. 13.

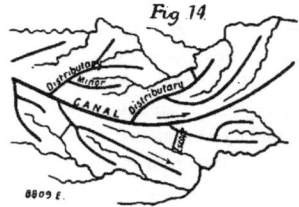

Fig. 14

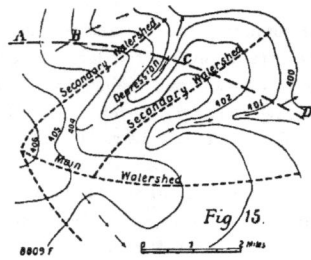

Fig. 15.

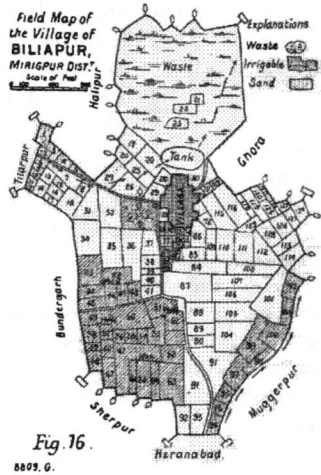

Field Map of the Village of **BILIAPUR**, MIRIGPUR DIST.

Fig. 16.

2. To avoid as much as possible heavy embankments or deep digging, as the former are always a source of anxiety, and in the latter the water is too far below the surface for irrigation purposes, and both are expensive.

3. To avoid passing through tracts of rotten or sandy soil.

4. To avoid crossing drainage lines as much as possible.

The method of aligning branches and distributaries on the watersheds (Fig. 14) gives the nearest approach to fulfilling these conditions, but no system, if slavishly adhered to, can give altogether satisfactory results. It will be asked why this system was not adopted earlier by canal engineers. The answer is that the existence of watershed lines connected with the main watershed of the province was not clearly understood.

In the sketches above referred to the drainage lines have been indicated in firm continuous lines as streams, but to the eye of an untrained observer the plains of the Do-āb appear perfectly flat. Often, indeed, the slope is not more than 6 in. in a mile. After a very heavy rainfall the plain, covered with a few inches of water, will have the appearance of a vast lake reaching for miles and miles. Watch this water as it subsides you will notice sluggish currents setting in certain directions. As it falls still more, long winding depressions will remain full of water. Follow these depressions in the direction indicated by the current and you will eventually arrive at the outfall into some ravine or stream. During the dry seasons, especially when the plain is covered with standing crops of varying heights, it is almost impossible to recognise the presence of these depressions, and quite impossible to tell in which direction rain water would flow in them. Fig. 15 shows the plan of a piece of ground, such as is often met with in the districts irrigated by the Ganges Canal. The dividing depressions are shown by arrows. The watersheds or spurs are indicated by the dotted lines, and these are the lines that should generally be adopted for distributing channels. If we plot sections for any of the dotted lines we shall find an almost uniform slope in the direction in which the canal water will flow. The result is that, with the judicious introduction of falls, the water surface in the channels may be kept at an almost uniform level with regard to the surface of the ground. But if we take any section, A, B, C, D, such as would be given by a line running nearly parallel to the main line, we shall have the depth of digging or height of embankment constantly altering. The drainage at B, C, and D will be intercepted, and would necessitate the introduction at those points of culverts to carry off the rain water.

The construction of a contour map showing the positions of the depression and ridges for a large tract of country is a work of considerable labour. No surveyor, however skilled, can follow with absolute certainty the lines of drainage during the dry season. He can obtain a great deal of information on the subject from the villagers. But such information is not always reliable. The natives are exceedingly suspicious, and look on any innovation with distrust.

In order to obtain accurate data for the compilation of a large scale contour map of the country the following steps are usually taken : The surveyor personally inspects the country during the rainy season, and marks down upon the village maps the direction of the flow of drainage water in each village. When these maps are put together, an accurate representation of the drainage system is obtained. This work involves great exposure during the most trying and unhealthy season of the year. Parallel lines of levels at intervals of a quarter of a mile or so will enable the contour lines to be drawn in. (Levels were taken 500 ft. apart in every direction all over the tract of country to the north of Roorkee, containing the first thirty miles of the Ganges Canal.) In India these levels may be taken during the cold weather, but most conveniently during the spring when the winter crops have been cut. This work requires great accuracy. The slope of a distributary bed is sometimes as low as 4 in. a mile. The greatest care must be taken in marking the formation levels of such a channel. A feature in Indian levelling is the length of the sights that can be taken. These are often 500 ft. or a furlong. Perhaps the greatest safeguard against inaccuracies creeping in is to make it a rule always to place the instrument exactly midway between the two stations. Surveyors in India almost always employ pegs driven flush with the ground to mark the stations. The tops of these are rounded and the native staff-bearers have no excuse for shifting their staves about or working them into the soft ground. It is difficult to get natives to hold the staves perpendicularly; they are therefore taught to wave the staff backward and forwards in the line of sight, keeping the bottom firm upon the peg. The lowest reading observed is of course that seen when the staff passes through the perpendicular, and is therefore the one taken. Adopting these precautions, and avoiding levelling in the middle of the day when the mirage renders the readings indistinct, the greatest accuracy may be obtained. Natives make very accurate levellers, but their results are not always trustworthy. Trial lines of levels are usually plotted from the angles taken with a compass attached to the level, but some engineers have now given up reading angles, and mark down the position of the station direct upon the village map. The position of a station may be easily recognised by the shapes and sizes of the adjoining fields.

IRRIGATION MAPS.

Mention has been before made of the village maps. They contain a great deal of useful information, and we now propose to show how a large scale map, which is essential to the working out of an irrigation project, may be prepared from these maps with the assistance of the village records.

The village maps, as originally made for the use of the civil authorities, are outline maps showing the village boundary and every field in the village. Each village has a separate sheet. Each field is distinguished by a separate number, by which it is always referred to in the village records. These maps are known in the Do-âb as "shejras." They are printed in the vernacular of the district, sometimes on paper, but latterly, as they have to stand a deal of rough usage, and as great accuracy is not an essential, on linen cloth. In most cases the different kinds of soils, such as rich, average, or sandy, are indicated by dotted lines of different colours running round the tracts.

The books that contain the description of the fields are termed "khusras." These maps and records are kept in the charge of an official whose duty it is to keep up all statistics concerning the village, and to enter in them any changes that may occur in the ownership or boundaries of the land. He has also other duties to perform, such as keeping registers of crops, births, deaths, &c. In fact the "putwari," as he is termed, keeps up a complete history of the village. The post is generally an hereditary one.

In addition to the information already afforded by the village map, the agricultural engineer for the construction of his large scale map requires to know what land is suitable for irrigation, what lands are to be avoided on account of the sandy or barren condition of the soil, or on account of their being swamped during the rainy season or already irrigable from wells or tanks. This information is obtained from the khusras, and transferred to the village maps. It is customary to surround the tracts already irrigated with an emerald green line. Generally speaking this will denote that canal irrigation is not to be introduced into such tracts. Lands swamped during the rain are coloured dark green, barren lands yellow, and sandy tracts brown. Good dry culturable land is left plain, and this plain area is that for which irrigation is to be provided. It is unnecessary to distinguish between rich and averagely good soil, as both are suitable to irrigation, and take about the same quantity of water.

As the engineer has already marked the drainage lines he has now got all the data requisite for the compilation of his map. An outline map of the required scale—say 4 in. to the mile—showing village boundaries only, is prepared, and all details are copied off the village shejras, which are generally to a scale of about 16 in. to the mile. Any mistakes in marking out the drainage lines that have been made will become apparent when the maps are put together. The map will now (with the exception of the dotted lines) have the appearance shown in Fig. 18, page 28.

It is as well to keep the details of the levelling on a separate sheet (Fig. 17). To obtain the contours parallel lines of levels are run two to four furlongs apart. Personal inspection will enable the contours to be laid down with accuracy. The watersheds are now marked in dotted lines, and these will generally represent the lines for proposed distributing channels.

Let us examine Figs. 17 and 18 with a view to determine the best alignment for minor distributing channels in the piece of country represented. We will assume that the position of the Hiranabad distributary, which is to supply the minor channels, has been already decided upon. For the irrigation of Bundergarh and Biliapur the line A B C (Fig. 17) is the best as far as levels are concerned—it has a good uniform slope, and is direct. But this line passes through the middle of a well-irrigated tract (Fig. 18) and would probably interfere with existing irrigation. The alternative line A D C is less direct, but is satisfactory as to levels, and passes almost entirely through dry culturable soil. This latter is, therefore, the line that will probably be adopted. The line E F (Fig. 17) is the watershed line for irrigating Hatipur. It crosses drainage near Titarpur, but this drainage is local, due to the pressure of a worn-down road, and E F is the true watershed. In Fig. 18, however, we see that this line passes first through sandy soil, then through a grove of trees, finishing up in waste unculturable soil, and it is evident from the smallness of the homestead of Hatipur, that the soil is poor and cannot support many inhabitants. It is, therefore, improbable that it will pay to construct the channel E F. Possibly it may be advisable to continue the line across the drainage line, providing a suitable crossing at F, into the village of Ghora, which appears to contain good culturable land. The line G H is a much more satisfactory one, it is on the watershed, has a good slope, and passes almost entirely through dry culturable soil.

The village of Bundergarh being almost entirely irrigated from wells, will in all probability be debarred from using canal water. This question of debarring villages or tracts of country from canal irrigation is important, and will be discussed later on.

We have now followed the process of compiling a complete irrigation map for a few square

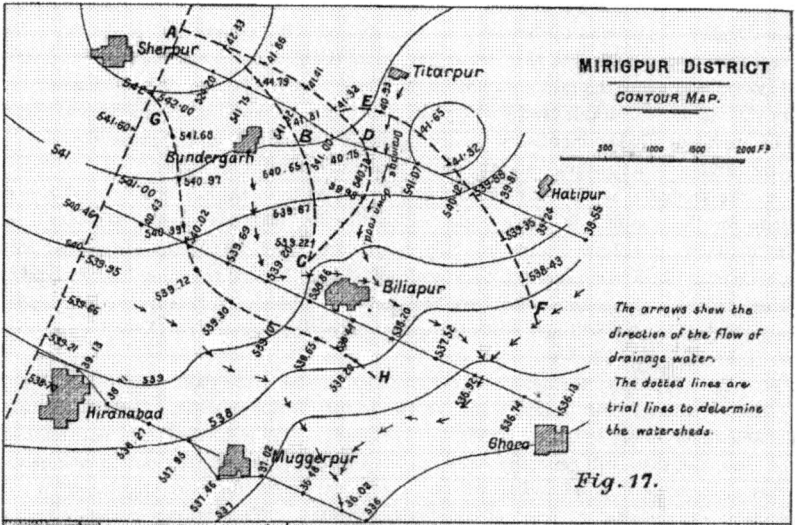

MIRIGPUR DISTRICT

CONTOUR MAP.

The arrows show the direction of the flow of drainage water. The dotted lines are trial lines to determine the watersheds.

Fig. 17.

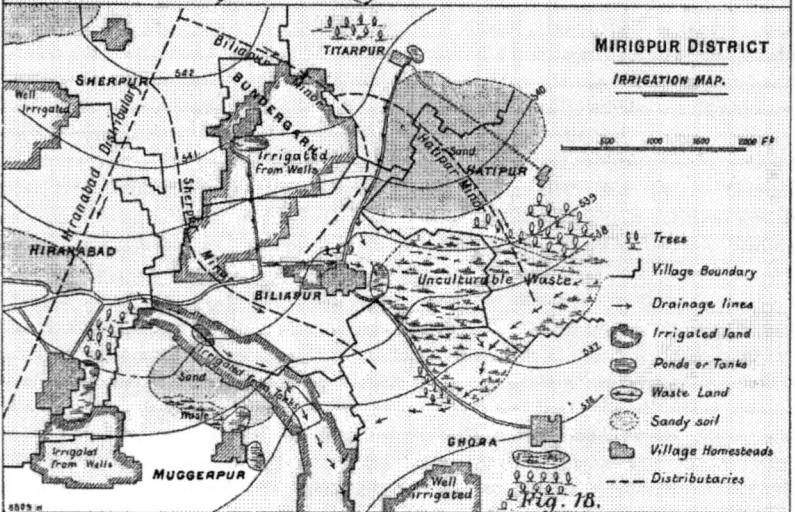

MIRIGPUR DISTRICT

IRRIGATION MAP.

Trees
Village Boundary
Drainage lines
Irrigated land
Ponds or Tanks
Waste Land
Sandy soil
Village Homesteads
Distributaries

Fig. 18.

miles of country. It will be seen that we have on the map not only all the data for determining the alignment of distributing channels, but also data from which the area commanded by each channel may be calculated, and consequently the size and section of the channel determined. The bed slopes of the channel will depend partly on the composition of the soil and partly on the level of the water surface in the supplying branch. It will be seen from the above that a great deal of personal inspection and earnest consideration is required before the engineer can finally lay down the lines for even a minor distributary.

WATER DISTRIBUTION.

In the last article the process was described of aligning a canal distributing channel so as to command the country as effectively and economically as possible. We now propose to describe the manner in which the water should be delivered to the cultivators.

We must, for the present, assume that the irrigation canal from which our supply is derived is completed, and the water delivered into a channel laid out on the principle described in the last article. We shall have the following conditions : a banked stream of water flowing along the highest ground, the water surface being about on a level with the ground, or somewhat above it. If the sidelong slope is steep it will be unnecessary to keep the water surface high (Fig. 19); but, if the country is very flat the water surface must, if possible, be kept several feet above ground so as to obtain the command of distant points (Fig. 20).

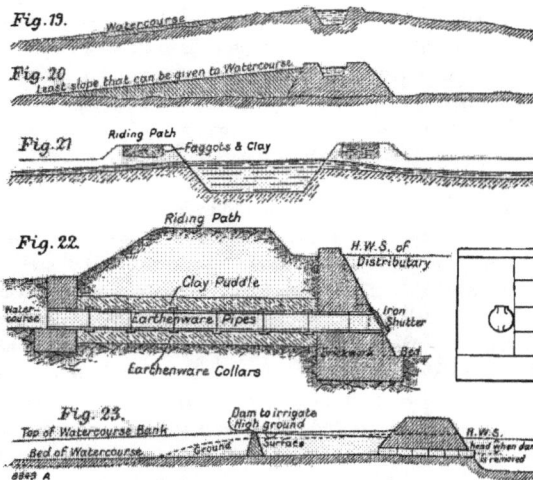

Fig. 19.

Fig. 20.

Fig. 21.

Fig. 22.

Fig. 23.

In order to distribute the water to the fields, outlets are provided in the banks of the distributing channel. The elementary form of outlet is a gap in the bank bridged over with sticks and clay (Fig. 21); this form possesses the advantage of simplicity of construction, and there is not much to get out of order. The highest form of outlet is some kind of module constructed of masonry and ironwork and giving a constant discharge of water under all circumstances. This is expensive to construct and difficult to maintain in good order, if it is so made that the natives are unable to interfere and tamper with the mechanism. A serviceable mean between these two extremes has been adopted as the most satisfactory form of outlet. It consists of earthenware pipes let into the bank and made water-tight by puddling or concrete (Fig. 22). The ends are defended and permanence secured by masonry blocks or terminals. Those on the inside of the distributary help to preserve the theoretical section of the channel, whilst the steps serve to gauge the depth of water. When a distributary is first opened it is customary to put in the outlets temporarily. The pipes are laid in puddle without any masonry accessories. After several seasons' experience those that give satisfaction as to size and position are made permanent. The diameters of the pipes are $4\frac{1}{4}$ in. and 6 in.; and in special cases 8 in., 10 in., and 12 in. pipes are used, but it is more usual now to place two or three 6-in. pipes alongside one another when a large discharge is required.

When once the water leaves the outlet the management of it is in the hands of the cultivators. The channels that ramify amongst the fields are called watercourses, in contradistinction to the distributaries, which are the channels maintained by Government, and they are constructed by the cultivators. Consequently, as a general rule, watercourses follow the boundaries of the fields, for the owners of fields cordially hate having them cut up by water channels, especially by those belonging to other people. Sometimes, indeed, it is found necessary to cut across a field, but it is always done grudgingly. If a cultivator refuse altogether to allow a watercourse to pass through his land the canal authorities may step in, and by compensating him, may take possession of the slip of ground required under the Land Acquisition Act. Sometimes a difficulty arises about supplying water to a distant village, the intervening villages refusing to allow the water to be taken through their lands. Unless an agreement can be come to the same course must be pursued, and the village that benefits by the use of the water must pay compensation for the land taken up. When such measures are necessary the watercourse is laid out and constructed by the canal officials and will go comparatively straight to its destination.

Road crossings are always a source of trouble to canal officers. The natives have no regard whatever for the comfort of travellers. The Do-āb is intersected in every direction by unmetalled village roads, which have been in use for hundreds of years, and are in consequence worn down often several feet below the adjacent fields. When we see the clouds of dust that roll off these roads as a herd of cattle passes along, we wonder that they are not worn much deeper. When the villagers wish to convey a watercourse over such a road they construct an earthen bank across and carry the water on that. Then comes the traveller in his heavy bullock cart; without remonstrance he climbs over this obstruction. His wheels will have cut through the banks of the water channel on the top, and he proceeds leisurely on his way leaving the water escaping through his wheel ruts into the road. Unless water is urgently required on the far side of the road no one will take the trouble to repair the bank, and the result is considerable waste and the road rendered almost impassable from mud and water. In new irrigation schemes the cultivators should be required to provide suitable crossings before ever the water is allowed to cross the road, or they should deposit sufficient money for the canal authorities to construct a suitable crossing.

The position of and the number of outlets in distributary banks are questions of importance to the engineer. Considerable difference of opinion exists as to the frequency with which the outlets should occur and their size. Whether it is more economical to have a considerable number of small outlets, or only a few large ones. The question of position must be decided to a great extent in accordance with the nature of the ground. There must, however, in such a matter, always be considerable scope for individual taste. For it is not one in which hard and fast rules can be laid down at head-quarters and rigidly adhered to. In some distributaries as many as ten or twelve outlets are to be found on one side in one mile, in others, the same amount of irrigation is done from one or two. In the latter case a greater loss of head is involved, for the fall required to convey water any distance in the tortuous and badly kept watercourse must be much greater than in the straight and well-trimmed Government channel. Three or four outlets in a mile on one side are the average number now found in a good irrigating country.

Fixing the sites for outlets depends on local circumstances, and they should be fixed on the spot, although they may be approximately fixed on the map to start with. While some men aim at mathematical accuracy in the relations of the size and number of outlets to the area to be irrigated, others, equally experienced, fix the sites and the sizes of outlets by eye, only roughly ascertaining the approximate areas to be irrigated. Without sacrificing a certain amount of head (which we can ill afford to do in the Do-âb) it is impossible to secure anything like constancy of discharge from an outlet. Fig. 23, which represents a very ordinary condition, shows the futility of expecting mathematical accuracy in these matters. When the lower fields are being watered there is a considerable head on the outlet and a good discharge, but when, in order to irrigate the high adjacent fields, the watercourse is dammed up, this head is destroyed and the discharge will be materially reduced. Outlets are usually placed at points where they will at once command the highest ground, but if this ground is so high as to necessitate heavy digging for the watercourse it is better to place the outlet about where the water surface and ground surface are on a level. The watercourse will then run more or less along a contour. Watercourses in deep digging are very wasteful, as they are often blocked up at some distance from the distributary. The channel remains full of stagnant water, and a great deal is lost by absorption.

DEBARRED TRACTS.

A question of the greatest importance in fixing the sites for outlets is whether land already provided with irrigation from wells should be provided with canal water or be debarred altogether. This question may be considered from two standpoints, the sentimental and the hard matter-of-fact money side of the question. Is it just to give water to people who are already provided for when there are large tracts of poor dry soil that might be brought under cultivation? Will it pay the canal better to irrigate the good clay soil which is commanded by wells, or to confine itself to the poor sandy soil that is so light that wells cannot be constructed at all? To get to the bottom of this question we must have some idea of the system of land tenure. In India the whole of the land belongs to Government, and the land revenue is its principal, in fact almost its only source of income. This revenue has been fixed at a certain percentage of the produce of the land, and therefore varies from field to field, with the character of the soil and the facilities for manuring and irrigation. The amount of revenue to be paid by each field is determined periodically for each district, and this is termed the land settlement of the district. These settlements are made at intervals of thirty years, and in the mean time, any difficulties that arise, as in the case of land from any cause going out of cultivation, are dealt with by the civil authorities upon the merits of the case.

One of the duties of the settlement officer, and the one that most nearly affects the canal engineer, is the determination of what fields can be supplied with water for irrigation from wells or other sources, the value of the land being considerably enhanced when such is the case. The circumstances will not admit of him making nice distinctions in the quality or permanency of the water supply. Such distinctions would lead to endless complications. Each field is merely assessed as " wet " or " dry," and a very great deal depends upon the personal character of the settlement officer, and the views held by him. Some officers may assess fields as " wet " that have a precarious supply of water from unstable wells. When these fail from drought or heavy rain the villagers suffer considerable hardship. The gradations from absolutely dry, unirrigable soil to rich, well-watered land, through that drawing its supply from inconstant or unstable sources are so very gradual that in this case again it is impossible to draw any hard-and-fast line. The work of the settlement officer is all the more arduous as the information afforded by the natives is not always reliable—indeed, they often go so far as to fill up their wells and plough them over some months before his visit, in order to get their land classed as dry.

Subject to the Crown, the land practically belongs in perpetuity to the landlords, who vary in rank and position from noblemen to simple cultivators. These are called the owners of the land. The ownership of land descends like any other property from father to son, and there being no primogeniture it is divided equally amongst the sons. These landlords in many cases sublet their lands to cultivating tenants. When a tenant has been in possession of a property for a period of twelve years, he acquires certain occupancy rights and cannot be ejected by the landlord.

It will be seen now that the improvement of property from any source is expected to benefit three parties—the tenant, the owner, and the Government. With the introduction of irrigation into an unirrigated property, its value becomes enhanced, and at the next settlement the land would be assessed as " wet," and an increased revenue taken from the owner, who will in turn enhance his tenant's rent. In order to tide over the interval between the introduction of canal water and the next settlement, Government makes it a condition of taking canal water that the landlords of unirrigated lands in return for increased fertility shall pay a tax termed owner's rate in addition to the water rate paid by the cultivating tenant. No tax is levied on the owners of property already assessed as wet, as they already pay the higher rate of land revenue to the Government.

It will be seen from the above that for the present Government gets a higher return for the water introduced into " dry " than for that introduced into the " wet " tracts. Thus, there are two very powerful arguments for only allowing canal water into tracts that are not already supplied with irrigation from wells, first that the canal water is meant to supplement the well irrigation of the province and not replace it; and secondly, that it is more lucrative, as Government obtains the owner's rate as well as the ordinary water rate.

But there are many large tracts of country where all the rich cultivable land is commanded by wells whilst all the unirrigated land is poor and sandy. If we introduce canal irrigation into such a tract and debar all the well-irrigated land from profiting by it, we cut ourselves off from all chance of watering the higher classes of crops that can only be grown on good soil, and confine ourselves to the poorer sorts which give such a small return to the cultivator that he will do all he can to avoid expending canal water on them. In the case of villages where the land is pretty equal in quality but only a portion commanded by wells, on the introduction of canal water the villagers will abandon their wells and employ the simpler method of watching the canal water running over their land. If those fields commanded by wells are debarred from using the canal water, the cultivators will confine their attention to the fields for which canal water can be obtained, and let their wells go to ruin in the hope of inducing the authorities to sanction canal irrigation in all parts. When wells are neglected, unless they are in exceedingly stiff clay or made of masonry, in fact, unless they be absolutely stable, they will soon collapse and go to ruin. After a lapse of time, when the next settlement is made, the settlement officer will find those fields originally assessed as " wet " quite dry, and will probably assess them as such, whilst those irrigated by the canal will be assessed as " wet." Thus the " wet " and " dry " areas will merely change places, and the object of debarring land will be defeated. Such cases as this can only happen where both the wet and dry areas belong to one community or village. The natural deduction seems to be that when any village is already well supplied with water from wells the whole of that village should be debarred from taking canal water, and that, when canal irrigation is permitted in any portion of a village it should be permitted in the whole village. Although it seems imprudent to debar certain areas of a village, still a good deal may be done to discourage the improper use of canal water by placing the outlets in such positions that they will command the " dry " areas with ease and the " wet " only with difficulty.

Figs. 24 and 25 give some idea of how the size of outlets may be fixed theoretically when their positions have been determined on. Fig. 24 is a diagram showing the area that it is proposed to irrigate from each mile for the distributary which is supposed to be 9½ miles in length. From this diagram we see that the greater part of the irrigation is to be done in the last few miles, whilst in mile three there is scarcely any at all.

Fig. 25 is a longitundinal section of the distributary, showing the slope of bed and the water surface and the ground level, and the positions of the outlets and the amount of water that can be discharged by each. The discharge of the distributary at its head should be equal to the discharges of all the outlets, and the discharge at any point should be equal to the volume discharged by all the outlets below that point. Such distributaries have been constructed, but their success is questionable. Were the conditions such that there must always be an equal demand for water along the whole length of the distributary, this system would work excellently, but such is seldom the case. In some instances local rainfall may occur, checking the demand in two or three miles only; or, supposing an indigo factory established near the head of the distributary, and the neighbouring villages all under indigo, whilst the villagers at the tail allow their land to lie fallow. There will be a heavy demand in the first few miles, but none towards the tail, where all the outlets will be closed. If a volume sufficient for the first few miles only is run in the distributary the water surface will fall so low that there will be insufficient head to supply the outlets, and if a full supply is sent down

c

all the water below the first few miles must be allowed to run to waste through escapes, or it will burst the banks. Something may be done to overcome this difficulty by constructing regulators at intervals in the channels, damming up the water by placing planks in them. In

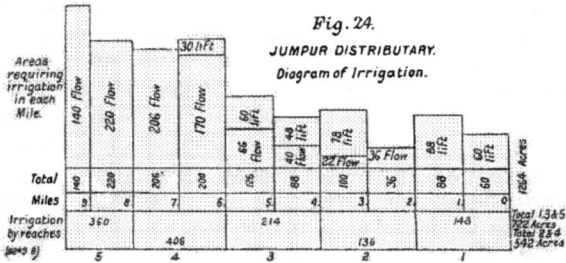

Fig. 24.

JUMPUR DISTRIBUTARY.
Diagram of Irrigation.

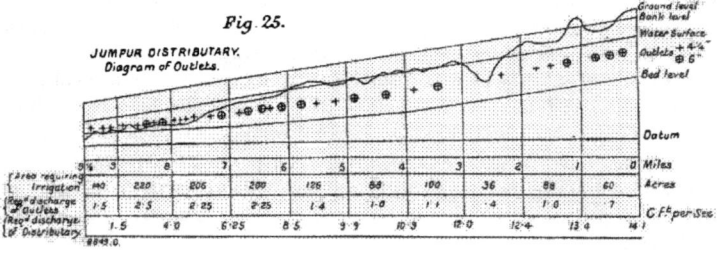

Fig. 25.

JUMPUR DISTRIBUTARY.
Diagram of Outlets.

channels where the water is at certain seasons laden with silt, these regulators cause heavy deposits and choke up the channel. They are of necessity isolated and only periodically inspected, so that they are very liable to be tampered with and improperly used.

TATEELS.

The most ordinary way of overcoming these obstacles to carrying on our irrigation intelligently is by having all the outlets very much larger than they are theoretically required to be and only permitting certain reaches to run on certain fixed days. This system is called "tateeling" (tateel is the Hindustani for an interval or holiday). It is customary to close

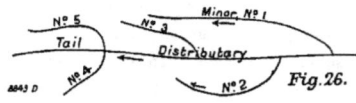

Fig. 26.

certain reaches for several days at a time and permit them to run for several days, and in order that the cultivators may know what to expect and have no excuse for breaking the tateels, certain days must be fixed for each reach and rigidly adhered to ; in fact, without a very rigid system, it would be impossible for irrigation officers to regulate the distribution of water at all, Thus in Fig. 26 reaches Nos. 1, 3, and 5 might be run on Sundays, Mondays, Tuesdays, and

Wednesdays, and Nos. 2 and 4 on Thursdays, Fridays, and Saturdays, the areas to be irrigated by the latter sections being about three-fourths that of the former.

When there are a number of minor distributaries branching off from a main distributary they may be tateeled like outlets. In Fig. 26, minors Nos. 1, 3, and 4 might be closed during one week, whilst Nos. 2 and 5 and the tail are closed during the next. Minor No. 1 is sufficiently long to require "tateeling" within itself. Say the first two miles may be closed for three days during its running week. The outlets in this portion will therefore only be open for four days in a fortnight, and must be correspondingly large. When irrigation officers have charge of a number of channels of this kind spread over a large tract of country, they are kept very much on the alert during the season of high demand, to see that every portion gets its proper share of water. And, not only must the cultivators get a certain number of waterings for their crops, but, to insure a good outturn, the waterings must be given just when most needed.

The tract of country under the charge, for purposes of irrigation, of an assistant engineer, is termed an irrigation subdivision, and is ordinarily about fifty miles in length and twenty miles or less in width, and is bounded laterally by two deep lines of drainage dividing it from other irrigating subdivisions. Two or three such subdivisions on the same canal form a division, which is in charge of an executive engineer, who usually has his head-quarters at some station lying in the district. A number of divisions adjacent to one another form a circle. There are only three circles in the North-West Provinces each in charge of a superintending engineer. The control of the whole of the irrigation of the provinces is vested in the chief engineer, who has his office at the seat of the local government, in the cold weather in the plains, and in the hot weather in the hills.

The work in an irrigation subdivision is exceedingly varied and interesting. Although the life is very isolated, and would appear to the uninitiated to be exceedingly monotonous, the canal officer seldom has any spare time on his hands, and such as he has is generally employed in shooting, hunting, or fishing, so that the life has considerable charm for men with a taste for outdoor work and sports. His inspection duties compel him to ride 10 to 20 miles almost every day. Besides the control and arrangement of the irrigation, as indicated above, there are always new works to be executed and old ones to be repaired. Projects for fresh schemes of irrigation and drainage to be prepared, and his plantations and experiments with crops and water, are a constant source of interest. During the hot season, however, the life is very trying. Irrigation officers are about the only class of men in India who have to remain out in camp during the hot weather. This is the season when there is the greatest demand for water, and subdivisional officers have to be more than ordinarily on the alert, and constantly journeying from place to place. When it is said that these officers remain in camp during the hot season, it must not be understood that they live in tents, for such a proceeding would be impossible. At about twelve miles apart all over the canals and on the main distributaries, rest-houses are constructed, and the engineer marches from one to another carrying his office and all his belongings on camels or in bullock carts. The subdivision is again divided into sections; usually there are six or seven sections, each in charge of a native subordinate, and under them again are native patrols who have beats of three or four miles in length, which they are expected to inspect every day, noting in their books any new fields that are being irrigated.

These patrols have to see that "tateels" are enforced, and that no damage is done to the channels or banks, besides keeping the latter in good repair. They are not supposed to interfere in any way with the watercourses or the distribution of water amongst the villagers, but they are often appealed to in cases of dispute, and no doubt receive many little presents for executing functions they have no right whatever to perform. But not more so, we believe, than do the police or any other Government subordinates. The natives have been accustomed to look on bribery as the legitimate means of attaining an end, and seem rather to prefer it to making a straightforward application. It is, however, being slowly but surely eradicated. The canal officers are now inundated with petitions, as the villagers have learnt that the surest way of getting a grievance redressed is by applying straight to the authorities, and not by bribing subordinates. Such a thing as offering a bribe to an Englishman is now almost unknown. These facts show that the native's ideas of honour and probity are growing more in conformity with our western notions.

CANAL HEADWORKS.

In selecting the locality for the headworks of a canal, it is an advantage to get high up the river, so as to command as much as possible of the tract that it is proposed to irrigate. The point selected for the head of the Ganges Canal is at Hurdwar, where the river passes through a gorge in the Siwalik range of the Himalayas previous to debouching on to the plains. This is as high up in the course of the river as it is possible to go in search of a canal head. Here the transition from the mountains to the plains is sudden. The plain runs up into the valleys and contours the spurs. It is like a monster that holds the mountains in its grasp; it grows and fattens on their decay and will eventually swallow them up and leave no trace. Then, when its source of nourishment is gone, it will, in turn, melt away and vanish in the sea.

This characteristic of the country, whilst it enables the canal to be taken off immediately the river leaves the mountains is not at all favourable to its maintenance or preservation. The débris brought down by the rapid disintegration of the Siwaliks have caused, and will continue to cause, grave engineering difficulties. These hills are composed of a red or grey sandstone, varying greatly in texture. In places it can be cut with a spade, in others it makes a building stone fit for the mason's chisel.

The river at Hurdwar, and for a few miles below, has the character of a torrent. It is studded with islands and sandbanks, between which the stream runs in a series of pools and rapids. The bed of these streams is composed of round boulders seldom more than about a foot in diameter. A walk of a couple of miles up one of the dry torrent beds behind Hurdwar will show us the formation of these boulders in course of progress. At the junction of the torrent with the Ganges the broad, flat, sandy bed is strewn with stones, similar to those in the great river. For a few hundred yards back, the slope of the torrent's bed is slight, for the river floods back up into it and hinder the rapid flow of water when the torrent is running in the rainy season, leaving heavy deposits of sand. As we proceed upwards, the bed gets steeper and narrower and the boulders larger and more irregular in form, while the banks are overhung with bamboo jungle. These torrent-beds are the high-roads by which wild animals descend into the plains at night. The tracks of deer are plentiful, and we may come upon the fresh prints of a tiger or a panther. After a walk of a mile or so a perpendicular wall of rock arrests us, and we are obliged to make a detour in order to reach the bed of the torrent above it. Here the channel becomes very deep and narrow ; the bamboos are replaced by scrub and long grass. The boulders are not much worn, and every here and there is a great angular block of sandstone that has only recently been detached from its parent rock, and has not yet commenced the descent that will, in a few years, leave it a small round boulder in the river bed. The ground is damp, pools of water lie between the boulders, and ferns and moss grow in the crevices of the rocks. It is as well to have a rifle with us, as we may chance to stumble on a tiger or a panther in the long grass ; but more likely a sambur stag or spotted deer will bound away out of our path. The last bit is steep, and the bed is choked with grass and jungle, and when, at length, we reach the summit, it is a relief to exchange the stifling ravine for the breezy hill-top. We can enjoy the cool air and the scene that is spread out around us like a panorama.

To the south and west stretches away as far as we can see, the dead level of the plains. In the tract immediately below us, which owing to its proximity to the mountains enjoys a copious rainfall, the country is green and wooded, and the forests, the rivers, and the hamlets are distinctly marked. Beyond, the plain is covered with dust, as with a canopy, which, whilst it conceals the features of the country, in no way protects the sweltering inhabitants from the sun's fierce heat. To the north is the valley of Dehra Doon, where the heat is never intolerable and where wild roses grow upon the hedgerows. Beyond the Himalayas rise range above range. On the summit of the nearest, at an altitude of 7000 ft., we can discern the white villas of Mussourie glistening in the sun. The highest snowy peaks beyond are Bunderpooch and Kidarnath ; although they are eighty miles away their height of over 20,000 ft. makes them appear to tower above us. A feeling of our own littleness takes possession of us. Our ordinary duties, our comings and goings seem futile and insignificant in the face of so much grandeur. We long to stop up here among the wild beasts and shake off the trammels of civilization. The anxieties about money and the desire for fame that occupy our thoughts within the four walls of our bungalow below, here seem mean and sordid. Even the value of the rupee sinks into insignificance.

The hardness of our rocky seat may bring us to recognise that all this expanse is made up of details ; and, with a revulsion of feeling, we should remember with pride that we have a part, no matter how insignificant, in the vast scheme of civilization, and contribute to its grandeur.

In this frame of mind we turn our attention to the scene immediately below us to the east, where the river, with all its islands and the works which it is our intention to study, are laid out as in a plan.

The first thing that will strike us in these works is the absence of any long weir or dam right across the river. We see, however—supposing our visit to be during the dry season when all the available water is being sent down the canal—a number of small dams connecting the islands with one another and with the main land. Some of these dams have a permanent character, some are embankments evidently of a temporary nature.

In constructing weirs across a river the object generally aimed at is to intercept the whole of the water during the season of low supply, and at the same time to present as slight an obstacle as possible to the passage of floods during the rainy season. This object is, in some cases, compassed by placing a permanent weir across the river, and providing it with gates which can be dropped during the flood season to allow of a tolerably free passage of the water ; in others, by constructing annually, as soon as the floods begin to subside, a temporary dam across the river to keep up the supply. The former method is adopted at Narora, the head of the Lower Ganges Canal, the latter at Faizabad, the head of the Eastern Jumna Canal. The works at Hurdwar are a combination of both these plans.

When the Ganges Canal was constructed the main stream of the river was along the left bank under the Chilla and Chandi hills, and in the dry season only a small trickle of water, encouraged by the excavation of short channels here and there, flowed past the sacred ghâts of Hurdwar. The condition now aimed at in the training works is, during the dry season, to send the whole of the volume past Hurdwar into the canal ; but at the same time to keep the main channel of the river during floods, to the middle and left bank ; and thus avoid all risk of the main body of the flood passing down the Hurdwar channel and bursting into the canal.

In Fig. 27, A is the Chillawala weir ; it is a permanent weir made of cribwork boxes filled with boulders. The outside layers are laid in mortar and carefully dressed off to form a level crest. It prevents water from passing down the left-hand channel during the dry season.

B is bund No. 1, a temporary dam made of wooden cribs filled with boulders to deflect the dry weather supply down the Hurdwar channel. This dam is reconstructed annually as soon as the floods subside in the autumn and swept away when they rise again in the spring.

C is bund No. 2 of shingle to intercept the leakage from bund No. 1.

D is bund No. 3 to intercept the leakage from bund No. 2.

E is the Hurdwar dam, a permanent work of boulder masonry to prevent the water that we have led into the Hurdwar channel from escaping down the channel at the head of the Bailwalla Island. It is provided with drop gates, and serves as an escape to regulate the supply in the Hurdwar channel.

F is the Myapur dam, provided, partly with drop gates and partly with lift gates, for regulating the depth of water immediately above the canal head and consequently the supply in the canal.

G is the Myapur regulator having lift gates for regulating exactly the quantity of water entering the canal.

These two last works are highly finished and form the head of the canal proper. Those above are rougher in character, but year by year they are improved and are assuming a more permanent and finished appearance, and the entrance to the supply channel at Bhimgoda, which is revetted for some distance on both sides, bids fair to rival Myapur, as the true head of the canal. The nose of the island opposite Bhimgoda and the head of the Bailwalla Island are also protected by revetments.

The annual construction of the bunds is a work of considerable interest, and a cause of much anxiety to the officer in charge of it. The work occupies several weeks, and during that time an upper subordinate of the canal department is stationed at Bhimghoda ; and the executive engineer in charge of the division usually takes up his quarters at Myapur, and constantly inspects the work.

As soon as the rains finish, generally in September, the river falls very rapidly, for the summer snows having all melted, the river has recently been drawing its large volume from the rainfall. It is generally important to be able to run a full supply in the canal immediately the rains cease, and therefore the immediate construction of the bunds is imperative. The occurrence of late floods is a cause of great anxiety. If heavy rains occur after the bunds are completed they will be breached and carried away, or else a large volume of water will be thrown into the Hurdwar channel and a great strain put upon the works at Myapur. If the flood occurs during the construction of the bunds the work is much retarded. Occasionally a heavy flood occurs in October, and several years ago the canal was threatened with destruction by a flood occurring after the construction of the bunds. Fortunately several barges were carried down against the Myapur regulator, and the arches becoming choked with trees and débris, resisted the entry of the flood into the canal; for the flood was so sudden and the head of water so strong that it was found impossible to work the gates. Such a large volume of water

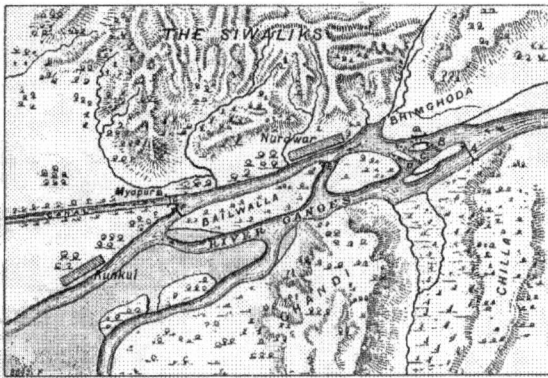

FIG. 27. HEADWORKS OF GANGES CANAL AT HURDWAR.

entering the canal would probably have meant the destruction of all the falls over which it passed, and possibly of the Solani aqueduct at mile 20, which would render the canal useless for some years. The canal might, however, have been relieved at mile 14, where there is an escape. The officer in charge of this part of the canal was prepared to blow up the head of this escape, so as to obstruct the escape of the flood as little as possible. The anxiety, therefore, with which the state of the weather and the rise and fall of the river are watched at this season can be appreciated.

The crop of indigo being cut during the rainy season, and the wheat and barley being sown shortly after its termination, there is a very prevalent custom of following the indigo crop with a crop of wheat or barley on the same ground. It is generally impossible to prepare the caked indigo fields for the wheat sowings without having recourse to artificial irrigation. And again, if the cultivators cannot get water early for irrigating the young corn they put off taking canal water in the hope of a plentiful rainfall at Christmas, a hope that too often fails to be realised. When this is the case it is bad, both for the crops and for the canal revenue. Bund No. 1 has to be laid in water from 10 ft. to 20 ft. in depth, and running with a very

FIG. 28. HURDWAR FROM BAILWALLA ISLAND.

great velocity. The bund is made of boulders, but if even the largest boulders are thrown into a stream of this kind the majority of them will be swept away. They are, therefore, encased in wooden crates (Fig. 29), and these are lowered into position from boats. The crates are laid from both ends simultaneously. At first only a sufficient number of boulders to sink the crate are put in. After it has been adjusted in position and securely lashed to its next-door neighbour it is filled up. The crates are made on shore, of sizes varying with the depth of water in which they are to be laid. The depths are obtained from a section prepared from soundings taken shortly beforehand. This section varies greatly from year to year. Some-

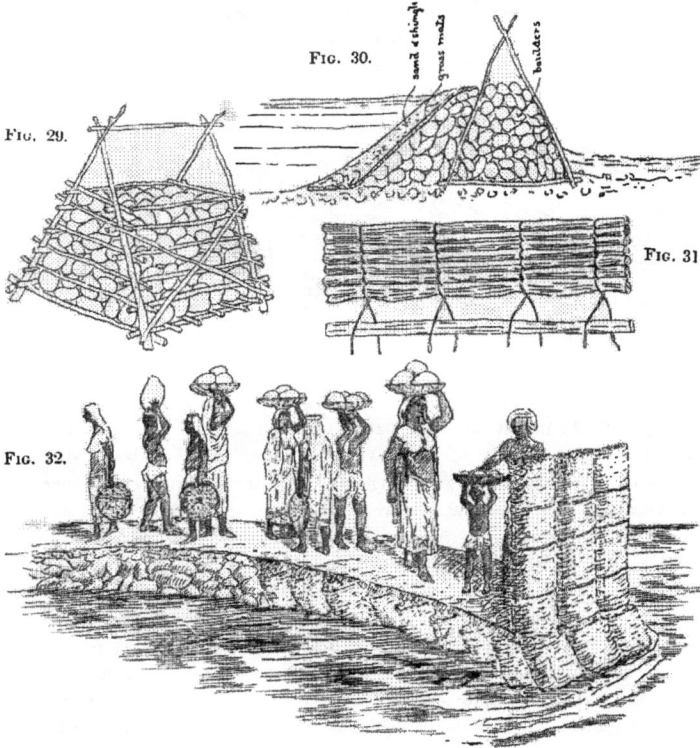

Fig. 30.

Fig. 29.

Fig. 31.

Fig. 32.

times bund No. 2 is made with crates, sometimes the depth of water is so slight that this is unnecessary. Bund No. 3 is a simple bank of shingle. In order to render boulder bunds as water-tight as possible grass mats are spread on the upstream face and covered with a layer of sand or shingle (Figs. 30 and 31). At the head of the Eastern Sumna Canal, where the depth of water is not so great, the boulders are inclosed in fascines made of a suitable length, and tipped over from the end of the bund as it proceeds (see Fig. 32). The mouth of the fascines is covered with a coarse netting.

As, on account of the stony bed and the velocity of the current, no anchorage can be got in the river, it has been found necessary for the construction of bund No. 1 to stretch a hawser across the river and work the boats, meant to convey boulders and crates, from that. By means of pulleys travelling on this hawser, and capstans on the boats, by steering against the current they can be moved about in any direction. The hawser is of immense thickness, and, with the appliances available, to get it across and stretch it tight is a matter of some difficulty. Hundreds of men are employed on this, but as they have to be collected for some days before the construction of the bunds so as to be in readiness, they might as well be employed in this as in doing nothing. The majority of the workmen come from the villages to the south and west of Hurdwar, and many of them return to their own homes every evening.

FIG. 33.

The craft available for the work are flat-bottomed native barges and a few iron barges. These latter are provided with derricks for laying the cribs. All these boats are towed up the river with difficulty from the canal to Bhimghoda. For inspection purposes there are two or three iron rowboats, but they get much injured from bumping on the boulders, and a good deal of inspection is done on "surnais." A surnai consists of a couple of inflated buffalo skins supporting a native cot or bedstead. (Fig. 33.) This raft will carry two persons and is pilotted by two natives who swim behind. How the buffalo is got out of the skin is a mystery, for there are no large cuts visible on the hides. Simply the mouth, eyes, and ears are sewn up, and the four legs, which stick up as the skin floats on its back, are tied round with string. The joints being not absolutely air-tight, the voyager will be alarmed by finding his supports getting flabby and the raft sinking gradually in the water. The surnai-walla, however, has his wits about him, and when necessary unties one of the legs, and putting all the power of his lungs into it quickly inflates the skin again. In crossing streams a good deal of leeway is made, but the raft is very handy to take out and carry across islands from one channel to another. Sometimes small rafts of gourds set in a framing of bamboos and string are used; and sometimes a number of elongated gourds are tied together into a kind of life-belt which is placed under the chest whilst swimming. These are called "tumris;" the tumri-wallas can travel at a great pace through the water.

To convey the workmen across the Hurdwar channel, a flying bridge, on the principle of the Rhine bridges, is employed; it consists of a country boat having a mast stepped slightly in advance of the centre; the cable, instead of being anchored, is attached to a rope stretched across the channel.

All the materials for the bunds must be stored the year before; for at this season—just after the rains—all the forest roads are closed, and the river is so high that the large boulders are not exposed. Supply channels No. 2 and No. 3 have usually to be dug out whilst the bunds are being constructed.

The completion of the bunds will send all the water in the river down the Hurdwar channel unless there be some still running over the Chillawalla weir. A bank of sand, run along the crest, serves to arrest this. As the river is very sensitive to rainfall in the hills, this supply will often be more than is required for the canal, and it will be regulated, principally, by escaping water from the Hurdwar dam, and from the Myapur dam. The former is provided with drop gates of a simple description. They are held up by chains attached to hooks on the gates; they may be unhooked by the blow of a crowbar, when the gate will fall. (Figs. 34 and 35.) There are several attachments used for drop gates on the canal works. Rapidity and

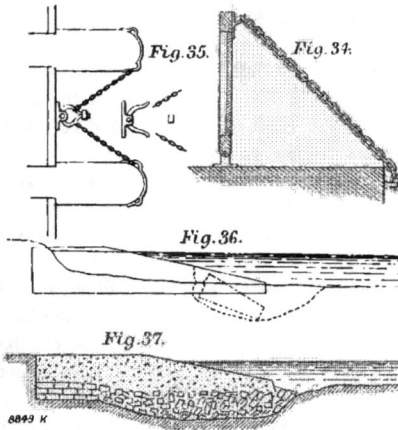

Fig. 35. Fig. 34.

Fig. 36.

Fig. 37.

8849 K

simplicity are the two qualities aimed at; for the floods rise very suddenly, and the gates and chains have to remain under water for months at a time. A simple form is employed on the Danauli escape, at mile 14 of the canal; when a nut is struck off with a hammer, the jaws fly open and the chains are released. No self-acting gates are employed on the Ganges Canal.

For the regulation of the supply in the Hurdwar channel gauges are placed in the river at Hurdwar, Bhimghoda, and at Raiwalla, a few miles higher up the river. These gauges are read daily, the gauge reader often swimming down the river on a tumri. The supply in the canal can be regulated to half an inch.

Opposite the Hurdwar dam are the Sacred Steps of Hurdwar. Here the Brahmins feed the sacred fish, fat, golden mahseer, that crowd round the steps jostling one another out of the water. The great annual fair, which is a horse fair as well as a religious festival, used to be held on the Bailwalla Island, which was connected with the main land by pontoon and boat-bridges erected by the Sappers and Miners from Roorkee and by the canal department. The sacred bathing-place is railed round to prevent the pilgrims crowding one another into the deep water beyond. English police officers regulate the traffic, sanitary arrangements are made under the direction of English doctors, and there is always a small camp of cavalry officers who come to buy remounts, and of visitors to see the fair. But these officials and visitors are swamped by the multitudes of natives, and the scene is still intensely Oriental in character.

The Bailwalla Island has but too often proved the centre from which the deadly contagion of cholera has spread into towns in every part of India. It was, until recently, assumed that this island was the best possible site for the fair. The soil consisted almost entirely of sand, it was isolated from the mainland, and swept at night by the "dādu," as the breeze is called that pours at night down through the mountain gorges on to the plains. During the day the heat expands the atmosphere of the plains, but as soon as the sun goes down, it contracts again, and the cool air of the mountains rushes in to fill the vacuum. This cool breeze, however pleasant in the hot weather, is most unhealthy to sleep in, especially in the autumn, when it passes over the swamps and marshes, filled with the decaying vegetation of the summer, that abound in the eastern parts of Dehra Doon.

Recent sanitary inspection of the site of the fair has led to the following conclusions. The sandy soil of the Bailwalla Island does not lend itself to the decomposition and dissipation of decaying animal matter in the same manner as culturable soil, in which this becomes absorbed into the crops that grow upon the spot.

The site of the fair has therefore been transferred to the west of Hurdwar and north of the canal, where the soil is cultivated and the site sheltered from the dādu. The horses and cattle can be conveniently watered at the canal and the dangers of the crowded bridges are avoided.

The islands in the river and the low valley land at Bhimghoda have been formed by the river at no very distant date; the surface of these lands is therefore about the height of the high flood level of the river. They are composed mainly of sand, consequently a great deal of care is necessary to protect them against being cut away during floods. Such a cutting away would upset all the arrangements for preserving the régime of the river. No spill of water, however slight, must be allowed across these low lands, as the sand very quickly cuts away, a channel is soon formed, and the island disappears. Indeed, whenever it is necessary to remove an island or sandbank from a channel, the only step that it is generally necessary to take is to cut a small channel straight through.

Spills across the low lands are prevented by marginal embankments, made a few feet higher than the highest flood mark to prevent their being topped, and by cross embankments joining the marginal banks to the high ground. These banks are made of earth or shingle and require constant supervision, as any unsoundness, such as an undetected rat hole, may in a single night cause an irreparable breach.

In order to protect the sides of the channels and prevent the marginal banks from being cut away laterally, revetments (Figs. 36 and 37) are constructed at the more important points, such as the head of the Hurdwar channel at Bhimghoda, and the head of the canal at Myapur. These revetments are made of boulders inclosed in cribwork or of rough boulder masonry strengthened by occasional layers of brickwork. This is too expensive a process to adopt for any great length, and in order to protect the greater portion of the river banks, projecting spurs are resorted to. These spurs keep the rush of the water towards the middle of the stream, leaving comparatively dead water near the banks.

When a spur is first put in the obstruction causes a very violent action, the bed is quickly scoured away and the nose of the spur breaks off (Fig. 36) and falls into the hole thus formed. Supposing the spur to be composed of heavy concrete blocks without mortar, and to be built up as fast as it falls in, after some time a permanent foundation will be formed, the upper portion may then be laid solidly in lime and neatly dressed off, without much fear of destruction. This is the principle followed in making spurs on the Upper Ganges. The upper portion of the best and most permanent spurs are made of concrete, but various materials are put in first to obtain a foundation, such as cribwork boxes 10 ft. square, filled with stones or concrete blocks. Some spurs, especially the longer ones, are made of a number of cribwork boxes laid close together.

Not only have the channels leading to the canal to be protected in this way, but the far sides of the islands must be attended to so that they may not be taken in flank. Some important spurs are located at a dangerous point on the south side of the Bailwalla Island, where the river in flood, turned by the rocky promontory at the foot of the Chandi Hill, makes a dead set on the island. Still further down, the town of Kunkul has to be protected by spurs, for should the town suffer at all, the mischief would surely be attributed to the canal works above.

The whole distance embraced by the training works is about five miles. The supervision of these works, which entails a great deal of responsibility, is usually entrusted to one of the most reliable upper subordinates in the irrigation department. As the fishing and shooting in the neighbourhood is exceedingly good the post would be gladly accepted by junior members of the engineer establishment.

Within the last few years a branch railway line has been constructed from the Oudh and Rohilcund line, and numbers of visitors, English and native, visit the place during the cold season.

GANGES CANAL HEAD.

Fig. 38 (see page 46) is a sketch plan of the head of the Ganges Canal at Myapur, as originally constructed. There is a regulating bridge across the canal head. The 20-ft. bays can be closed by strong wooden gates. There are two gates in each bay, lifted by chains and capstans worked by hand. The dam across to the Bailwalla Island consisted of a floor 3 ft. in thickness, with a deeper curtain along the face, made of boulders laid in mortar. Upon this floor stood the brickwork piers, 10 ft. apart, the intervals being closed by drop gates.

Experience has shown that both the general design and the details of these works were not as satisfactory as might be. During floods, when the regulator gates are closed, the pocket A becomes a receptacle for silt and débris brought down by the river. After the floods a shoal is left which obstructs the entry of water into the canal. In order to force the water over this shoal and keep up supply, the surface of the water in the river above the dam has to be raised considerably above the height for which the dam was originally designed. The piers not being sufficiently high to effect this, the brick pillars shown in Fig. 39 have been built. Planks let into grooves bring the gates up to the necessary height. This raising of the water surface above the dam has led to difficulties in getting at the gate fastenings, which were originally designed to be just above ordinary high supply. This is a very serious fault, as the gates have often to be worked at night, and in order to get at the chains it is often necessary for two men to cling on to the waistband of a third, whilst he dives below the water surface to reach the

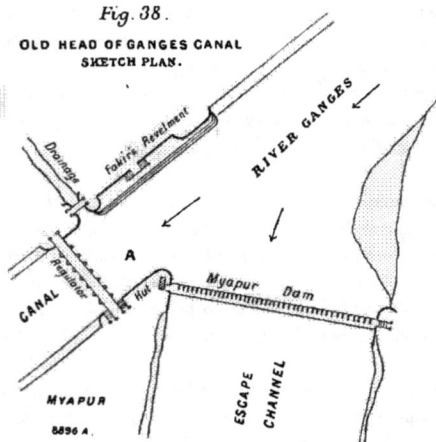

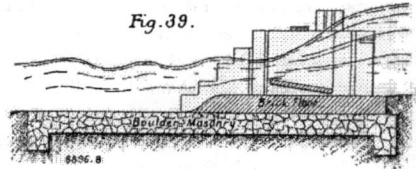

Fig. 38.

OLD HEAD OF GANGES CANAL
SKETCH PLAN.

Fig. 39.

fastenings. If we put ourselves in the position of these men, standing on the piers, above their knees in rushing water, upon a pitch-dark night, drenched with spray and with the cold wind from the mountains blowing down upon them, the necessity for reform will become apparent.

The communication between the Bailwalla Island and the mainland is kept up, except during floods, by sleepers laid across the tops of the piers. They are only planks about a foot wide, and when the water is rushing through the bays the passage is a nervous one for those unaccustomed to it. A few years ago there was some hundreds of coolies working on the island breaking up ballast for the remodelling of the dam. A sudden flood carried away the sleepers, covered the dam piers and cut them off from communication with the mainland. They were obliged to remain without shelter on the island for several days, and with only such provisions as could be sent across to them on native rafts.

Again, the gates of the dam have been found to be too small and those of the regulator to be too large. The floods bring down with them a good deal of floating timber; in fact, they are taken advantage of by timber merchants to float down the immense trunks of pine trees for which, at ordinary times, there is insufficient water. The shock from one of these striking the dam is very great, and every year several of the brick pillars are knocked off and the piers themselves much damaged.

When a great log sticks crossways against the dam it gathers to itself more logs, and very soon a dangerous obstruction is formed which it is very difficult to remove.

Such is not the case with the regulating bridge across the canal, for during floods there is a dead water above it. But the great size of the gates, 20 ft. by 6 ft., makes them exceedingly difficult to raise or drop against a large head of water. The regulator is not provided with a lock, so that boats can only be towed through at certain seasons when there is no head against the regulator.

For the above reasons it has been resolved to remodel the canal head on the lines shown in Fig. 40. The part of the dam nearest the regulator has been converted into sluice gates having 20 ft. openings to admit of the passage of large logs, and spanned by arches so that the

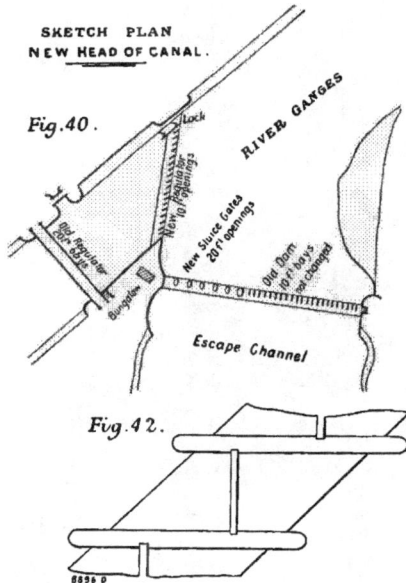

SKETCH PLAN
NEW HEAD OF CANAL.

Fig. 40.

Fig. 42.

gates may be worked from a powerful travelling hoist from above. A regulator is to be built at right angles to the dam, so as to allow a clear scour down its face and prevent the accumulation of silt in front of it. The gate openings, not being required to pass large logs, are to be 10 ft. in width and the gates worked from a roadway borne on arches above. The regulator to be provided with a lock at the northern end.

A point of difficulty in designing the regulator is the acuteness of the angle that it makes with the axis of the canal. It has been assumed that it is advisable for the river water to enter the canal in a direction parallel to its axis. No one will combat the principle involved, but when the serious skew of the arches and the difficulty of fitting the gates into them is considered, it is very doubtful whether a straightforward square structure, although it would cause more action in the water entering the canal, would not be preferable. A much greater turmoil

Fig. 41. Regulation Works at Head of the Ganges Canal, Myapur.

than would be caused by the waters entering through square arches is caused whenever the gates are partially closed, and the water has to rush into the canal beneath them.

The design at present fixed upon is a double-storied skew bridge. The lower story serves for sluice gates, the upper story arches are closed by dead walls on the upstream side. This story is merely to give height to keep out the floods, and to contain the gates when raised.

The grooves for the gates being on the square, the arches are cut in twain, and each resolves itself into two splay arches. Of these splay arches one abutment is only about 5 ft. in length, whilst the opposite one is about 13 ft. (Fig. 42). It seems questionable whether it would not be advisable to replace the upper story arches by simple girders to carry a roadway

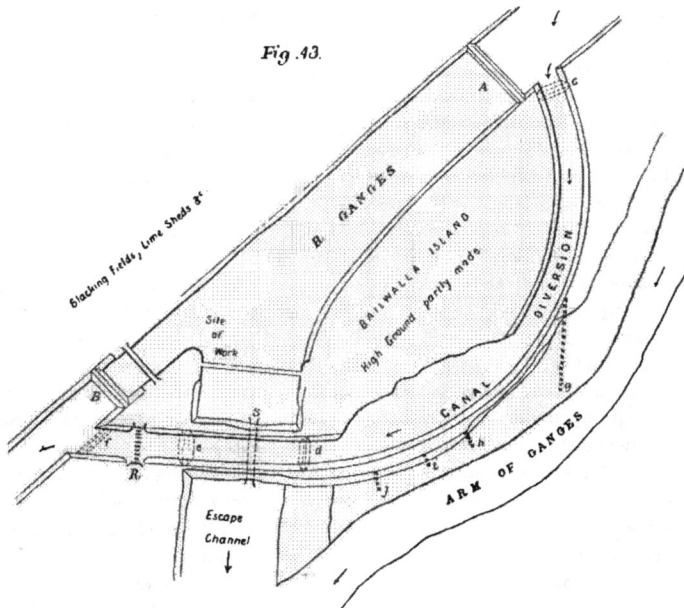

Fig .43.

for the traveller (traffic across the canal is already provided for by the old regulating bridge) and to add width to the lower story. The dead walls would still be required in the upper story.

Were the water impeded in its entry into the canal, by having to find its way through square arches, there would be a loss of head, but with the gain in head due to the abolition of the silt bar across the mouth of the canal, we can afford to lose a few inches if necessary. The piers on the down stream side might be provided with curved tails to guide the water into the direction of the axis of the canal. The wear on these piers would be nothing in comparison with that upon the piers and flow of the dam when floods rush over.

The remodelling of the dam and regulator was taken in hand in the winter of 1882, but

D

owing to a series of unexpected hindrances has not yet been completed, and is at present in abeyance. Even isolated engineering works, all over the world, are often subject to delays and hindrances from external circumstances having nothing to do with the actual constructive difficulties of the works themselves. And this is especially the case in public works in India, where the whole of the public works being under the Government, the interests of one branch of work has often to be subordinated to that of a more urgent work. For instance, the interests of many works that, at another time, would be considered urgent, have recently been subordinated to the construction of frontier railways. If we follow out the construction of the remodelled dam and regulator we shall get a very good idea of how isolated works are carried out in India, and the hindrances to which they are subjected.

As it was a necessity to keep the canal running continuously whilst the head was laid dry for remodelling, a diversion became necessary. The height of the ground to the north of the canal head was against the construction of a diversion on that side. It was therefore designed as shown in Fig. 43, which shows the diversion as completed. The site of the work was to be drained by the syphon S in the bed of the escape channel. The two high banks across this channel were to be of puddled clay mixed with boulders; that on the downstream side being kept low and pitched with boulders so as to afford a safety valve if necessary. The temporary regulating bridge was to be closed with planks in grooves; one bay to be 20 ft. in width, so as to take the gates from the old regulator and admit of the passage of boats. The bunds A and B are to keep the river and canal water respectively out of the works.

The excavation of the diversion and the construction of the syphon and the regulating bridge R, were completed during the spring of 1883, and strong boulder bunds put in at c, d, e, and f to keep out river water during the high floods which would commence in May. A long cribwork spur at g and smaller ones at h, i, j served to protect the diversion bank from the danger of being washed away during the river floods. Boats for the construction of the bund A had to be brought up and moored idly during the rains, so as to be in readiness to commence work as soon as the floods commenced to subside (see Fig. 44).

The materials for the work were collected and stored on the high ground to the north of the canal and upon the Bailwalla Island. It was proposed to complete the banks of the diversion and pass the water through it immediately on the completion of the rains (September, 1883). Unfortunately, however, the full supply of heavy granite blocks from Delhi for the floor of the regulator could not be made certain of in the time, and it was resolved to postpone the construction of the new regulator and merely to reconstruct the dam during that season. To effect this it became unnecessary to divert the canal, and a strong cribwork and boulder bund was run from A to B, Fig. 45. All water regulation had then to be done from the Hurdwar dam, a mile above this point. The remodelling of the dam was completed by the following spring (1884) before the river commenced to rise from the melting of the snows. With the rise of the river, the work had to be held in abeyance and the staff dismissed to other duties. On the termination of the rains of 1884, the necessary stone having meantime been collected, the construction of the new regulator was to have been commenced, and the work of getting the diversion completed was commenced with earnestness. Just, however, as the work was getting into full swing and labour collected from all directions, on the 4th of October, a very heavy rainfall occurred which caused heavy floods. An especially serious flood occurred in the River

Kali, carrying road and railway bridges before it, and partially destroying the Lower Ganges Canal aqueduct at Nadrai. This accident rendered a part of the Lower Ganges Canal entirely dependent for its supply on the old Ganges Canal. With everything, therefore, depending on

Fig. 44.

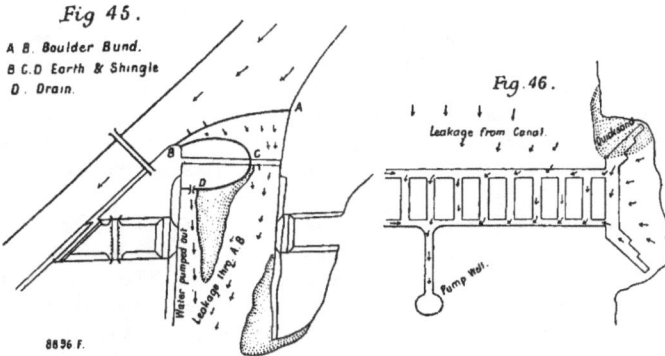

Fig 45.

A B. Boulder Bund.
B C.D Earth & Shingle
D. Drain.

Fig. 46.

Leakage from Canal.

Pump Well.

Water pumped out.

Leakage thro' A-B.

88 96 F.

the reliability of the supply at Myapur, it was not deemed prudent to risk intrusting the whole water supply of the province to a temporary diversion and a temporary regulator. The work was, therefore, postponed indefinitely.

A short description of the materials used, and the methods employed in constructing the Myapur dam, may be interesting as typical of the way in which works of this kind are carried on in out-of-the-way spots in India.

The staff employed immediately upon the work were an assistant engineer and two European subordinates, the general supervision of the work being in the hands of the executive engineer of the northern division of the Ganges Canal, the work lying within his district.

The pumping required for the foundations was done by centrifugal pumps driven by portable engines. These engines were brought along the canal bank from Roorkee, where the Ganges Canal Foundry and General Depôt is located.

All excavation was done by hand, the foundations of solid concrete on a good shingle bottom being laid comparatively dry by pumping.

The masonry work was of two kinds, boulder masonry and brickwork; the former was mainly employed in temporary works and in revetment walls of great thickness, the latter in permanent work, where a combination of strength and lightness is essential. The lime employed was of two different kinds; hydraulic lime made from the "kunkur" limestone of the plains, burned at Jaoli, some forty miles down the canal, and fat white lime, burned higher up the river from limestone boulders selected from the river bed. After the kunkur is burned into lime it is still so hard that it requires to be ground in a mortar mill before it can be used. This is usually done dry, and then the ground lime is used without slaking. The white lime on being slaked falls into fine powder and requires no grinding. When mixed with a proper proportion of powdered brick dust, ground from slightly underburnt bricks, this lime makes a good hydraulic mortar, which, though slower setting than the kunkur mortar, becomes just as hard and durable.

The temporary syphon, which required rather weight than strength, was built, up to springing, of boulders laid in a coarse mortar of sand, shingle, and lime, the arch being of brickwork.

The foundations of the temporary regulator were also of round boulders, but for the piers, which are high in proportion to their thickness, split boulders were used. These boulders are generally split into three pieces by blows from a heavy axe; they split easily when struck properly in the direction of the grain of the stone. The sharp edges of the pieces give a much better grip to the mortar, and the flat pieces can be coursed better than round stones. Bands of brickwork at every 3 ft. or 4 ft. in height give strength to the work and preserve the accuracy of the form of the piers. The cutwaters of the piers and the gate grooves are also of brickwork.

The foundation for the piers, abutments, and curtain walls of the temporary regulator assumed a gridiron form (Fig. 46), and as this could be only drained in one direction and the quantity of water to be dealt with being very considerable, some difficulty was experienced in laying the boulder masonry without getting the lime washed out. Could the foundations have been started at the extremities of the abutments and worked gradually towards a centre drain there would have been less trouble, but the time was exceedingly limited, and it was necessary to have the work going on in a number of trenches at the same time. Masons sat in the trenches, whilst streams of coolies brought boulders and mortar from above; the work was roughly coursed and the mortar put in more like grouting. In many places drain pipes had to be laid under the masonry in progress to prevent the water from heading up on the upstream side; when no longer required the mouths of these drain pipes were closed with bags of hydraulic lime quickly covered with concrete. A bad quicksand at one abutment gave a great deal of trouble, causing slips into the excavation. Timber frames were sunk through this on to the firm ground below, the sand removed and quickly filled with boulder masonry. The floor of the temporary regulator was finished off by brick on edge.

The old floor of the dam consisted of boulder masonry 3 ft. in thickness. The foundations under the new piers were to be 6 ft. in depth. It was at first proposed to remove the old floor altogether, but it was found to be so exceedingly tough that it was determined to allow as much as possible to remain. The floor was therefore broken through at intervals, and trenches for the new foundations excavated at these places. The shingle foundation was so sound that it did not slip away at all from under the slabs thus left. The breaking through the old floor

Fig. 47.

was a most laborious occupation, as it was so tough that the boulders had to be cut out with chisels and sledge hammers one by one. Explosives could not be used for fear of injuring the portions it was designed to retain. The trenches were filled with concrete made of two parts of stone ballast, broken so as to pass through a 1-in. ring, and one part of kunkur lime. The concrete was consolidated by ramming by hand. The same difficulty was experienced with the trenches as described above for the temporary regulator. Sometimes the concrete had to be put into very wet places, and swung about like a bog until all the water was driven out by determined ramming.

Wherever old and new work met, the joint was most carefully made, the old work being cleaned and damped and plastered with fine lime. The head of water close by, and the porousness of the shingle foundation, made it necessary to ram layers of quick-setting concrete one upon another as rapidly as possible, to prevent, by sheer weight, the formation of springs. If any patch of concrete were left overnight of less than a foot in thickness, it would be found in the morning full of holes with water bubbling through, although the water surface on all sides was kept down to the bottom of the concrete. This power of the slabs to collect water from a distance affords an excellent example of how the beds of clay lying beneath the ground surface throughout the Do-áb collect water for the supply of wells sunk down upon them. Of course the strength of these springs was minimised by keeping the water in the foundations as low as possible by pumping. A deep trench on the upstream side, kept dry, was found most valuable (see Fig. 48).

The last portion of the foundations to be constructed was an upstream apron, 2 ft. in thickness. For a day or two after this was made, the upstream drain was kept dry. This apron was made with slow-setting mortar, not with kunkur lime, but this mortar, if given time, is quite capable of setting under water. After a couple of days it was supposed that if the pumping was discontinued the drain would fill up, and the apron being covered with a few inches of water, there would be no pressure to hinder the mortar from setting. The apron was therefore covered with sand and the drain filled up, the downstream side of the work being kept quite dry. Immediately a number of springs burst through the apron, the drain had to be re-opened, and pumping renewed until the work was repaired and thoroughly set.

The concrete for the foundations was mixed wet on floors laid out above, and there being considerable competition amongst the natives supplying it, a sharp look-out had to be kept to see that it was properly mixed.

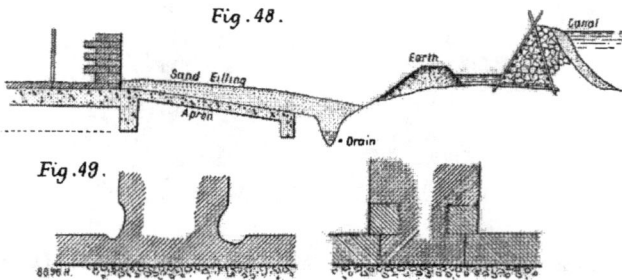

Fig. 48.

Fig. 49.

Between the piers, and extending a few inches under them, is a flooring of heavy granite blocks brought from Delhi. The lower foot of the piers is also made of granite to guard against the wear that is occasioned by boulders rolling along the floor, Fig. 49. The old piers of the dam are much worn at this point. In several places the floor of the old dam just above the piers has been churned into holes 3 ft. in diameter and 3 ft. in depth. There is always a large boulder or two at the bottom exactly like the glacier mills in Switzerland. To prevent this action, blocks of granite are let into the apron just above the piers.

The granite flooring only extended as far as the ends of the piers, and after the first rainy season's floods had passed through the new dam, the concrete talus was found to be much cut up. The granite blocks require to be extended some distance further. The old dam floor requires constant repair, and it seems as if nothing but a heavy granite flooring can stand, not the rush of water, but the action of the boulders, which during heavy floods may be heard rumbling along the floor from the banks.

WORKS.

In the last article the general design of the new head works of the Ganges Canal at Myapur was described, and some details given regarding the foundations. Some description of the way of carrying on the work, especially with reference to the part played by the natives, though matters of every-day occurrence to engineers in India, may interest those who have not had that experience.

Those whose engineering work lies more in the accurate designing of important structures in accordance with theoretical principles will be amused at the variety of the practical trifles that make the canal officer's life extremely interesting.

The irrigation engineer's profession comprises several distinct branches:

Administrative work, keeping his establishment under proper control, employed in the most efficient manner, and at the lowest possible cost.

Revenue work, including land measurements and control of the distribution of water so as to get the highest possible efficiency out of it.

Clerical work, including the framing of estimates and scrutinising the expenditure in every branch, and keeping accurate and exhaustive accounts.

Surveying for possible developments of irrigation and for constructing record maps.

General inspection of channels, masonry works, plantations, and navigation.

Practical engineering work, such as designing and supervising the construction of new works or the remodelling of old ones.

Interests as widely different as these in character have of course to be dealt with in all branches of engineering, but usually it only falls to the lot of those who reach the highest points in their profession to deal with them in their relations one to another. The actual work is carried on by men who are virtually specialists, and devote themselves to one branch only of the profession. The great charm of the agricultural engineer's work is that, from the very outset, he may identify himself with each and all of the interests enumerated above. When a new bridge is to be made in his subdivision the assistant engineer should be able to design and construct it. Should a survey be required the assistant engineer can do it. He must be versatile and on no account devote himself to one branch to the detriment of his other duties. Of course, most men prefer one particular branch, and make more or less of a study of that, but it would be a melancholy sight to see a man who has a taste for accounts and economy sacrificing the efficiency of his establishment or the thoroughness of his work, to his dread of spending a few rupees or exceeding an estimate, and it would be equally painful to see a man doing the best possible work with a disregard for economy or with a slipshod system of accounts that cannot fail to give dissatisfaction to the authorities.

When large works have to be undertaken canal engineers are deputed to perform special duties, and they are taken away from their revenue and other work to devote the whole of their energies to the work on hand ; but they are only specialists for the time being, and the officer who has been employed for a couple of years on supplying lime and materials for a large work, wrestling with petty contractors, and combating cheats on every side, will return with renewed vigour and interest to his plantations and nurseries, or to his work among the indigo fields.

The remodelling of the head of the Ganges Canal at Myapur is a good example of the kind of practical engineering work that occasionally falls to the lot of irrigation officers, and rouses them up when they are beginning to get a bit stale amongst their cornfields and their earthen channels. Most of the forms of labour that are employed by engineers in India were brought into requisition in this work, which, though not a large one, was characterised by a considerable degree of variety.

Although usually materials are collected and the work carried on under the immediate supervision of the officer in charge, contractors are resorted to to a large extent, and the lower in the social scale the contracts can be carried (the more they can be brought into the form of piecework, where the labourers are given an interest in the results) the greater efficiency we shall get out of every one concerned. The people on any work should be divided into two sections, on one side the contractors and labourers who actually supply the materials and do the work, and who are anxious to finish quickly, so as to realise as much profit as possible in the shortest time ; on the other the engineers and their overseers, who have no pecuniary interest in the work, but who, as paid servants of Government, are anxious to get the best possible value for their employers.

The question is occasionally raised whether it would not be advisable to give engineers some pecuniary interest in the economical construction of the works under their control. This is, probably, the very last thing that Indian engineers would desire ; they are often placed in isolated situations where their actions are quite free from any control of scrutiny whatever, and in these positions engineers often do their work more thoroughly and conscientiously than when under the eye of the authorities, and self-interest and desire for applause and promotion might be considered incentives to hard work.

They work hard, first because they are not driven ; because they are trusted and feel their responsibility, and because the native population and workmen look on them as directly representing the Government in that particular branch of administration which brings them into contact with one another.

These are the traditions of canal engineering. Absolute good faith in all matters of contract ; instant rejection of all work or materials not the best of their kind ; consideration for the losses of contractors due to unavoidable circumstances ; the power and the will to punish when occasion requires, and a cheerful assumption of responsibility by an officer for all he does or says.

The brick-burning at Myapur was done by a large European firm of contractors. In anything that involves the manufacture of materials at the site of a work, it is invariably best to employ a responsible firm, with sufficient capital to tide over temporary losses due to adverse seasons or some such causes. One of the somewhat recently constructed canals is littered with useless brick-kilns, and the stock returns oppressed with valueless underburned bricks for want of the recognition of this principle. Bricks were required in the greatest possible haste, and petty contractors presented themselves prepared to supply bricks up to specification if they only had enough capital to start with. Advances were made them, and the work proceeded satisfactorily. When, however, the bricks turned out underburnt and were rejected, the contractor, having spent his advance, and being heavily in debt to his labourers, had no alternative but to decamp and leave his inadequate securities to meet their fate or do the same. Occasionally the engineer only wants such a small quantity of bricks that it is not worth the while of a large firm to take up the contract. His best plan is then to burn them himself, employing daily labour ; they will cost more than they would if supplied by a big contractor with his experienced staff, but there will not be the same fear of a stingy supply of fuel as with the petty contractor. The kilns used at Myapur were Bull's patent trench kilns, for the use of which Government has paid a royalty, which entitles it to use these kilns on any works that it pleases.

These kilns are simple trenches, about 14 ft. in width, in which the bricks are stacked loosely but systematically, so that a thorough draught may be maintained in the direction of the length. The kiln is divided into chambers by leaving intervals of a couple of feet in the stacking at convenient distances. Numbers of vertical flues are left in the stacking for the introduction of fuel. The draught through the kilns is maintained by placing iron chimneys above certain of the flues, the rest being closed by iron plates, and a coating of ashes spread over all keeps in the heat. The chimneys are not placed immediately above the bricks that are being burnt, but some distance in advance, so that the hot air from the burning bricks is utilised in raising the temperature of those about to be fired. When these kilns are circular or oval in plan they are called perpetual kilns, for the process is continuous. As burned bricks are taken out behind, fresh ones are stacked in front ; the chimneys are constantly moving on, and the firing follows them (Fig. 50).

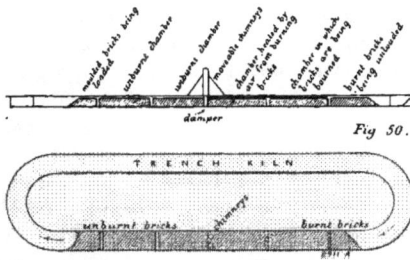

Fig 50.

In the piers of the Myapur dam only the hardest bricks were used, and for the face work only the dark, overburnt, vitrified bricks. These overburnt bricks being somewhat thinner than those used in the hearting, it became necessary occasionally to chip the bricks in the latter to preserve the accuracy of the coursing. The bond used was English, with an occasional herring-bone course. The mortar consisted of white lime and "soorkee," or powdered bricks, and the work was pointed very deeply with Portland cement. Masonry that has to stand the action of water must be laid with the greatest possible care ; almost every course is inspected, for the native masons are no better than they should be, and it would not go at all against their consciences to lay the bricks without any mortar at all. It is a good thing to occasionally pull down a piece of work to see that it is all right inside. The masons can then never feel certain that their work will not be opened and examined.

The bricks, before being laid, are soaked in water, and care must be taken that the mortar is not too wet, for the men are fond of doing sloppy work. New work has to be kept constantly wet for several days after it is built. If the lime sets too quickly it powders and separates from the bricks. The young engineer, set to superintend masonry work in India, is apt to think that the masons know as much about it as he does, and to let them have their own way; but he will soon find that, although they have been for years and years drilled in the way they should go, the instant they are allowed to do as they please they will lapse into the most slovenly manners.

The granite flooring of the dam and the noses of the piers were laid in a mortar composed of one part sand, one kunkur lime, and one Portland cement, and the heavy floor stones were clamped together, the clamps being run in, some with lead, some with sulphur, and some with Portland cement,

The stacking fields for materials such as stones and bricks, the lime sheds, and lime and " soorkee " mills, together with the storehouse and the engineer's office, were situated on the north side of the canal. In order to convey materials to the work a narrow gauge tramway was laid down having a number of branches, ramifying through the stacking field. Crossing the regulating bridge, it ran down a steep gradient to the work.

All the stones for the regulator and dam were first collected in the stacking field, dressed, and put into position there, before being carried to site. A good deal of trouble was experienced with the stone dressing, the locality being isolated, and expensive for natives. Besides which the stone was very much harder than anything the masons were accustomed to deal with. Before giving out the stone dressing in contract it was deemed expedient to discover, if possible, what the dressing ought actually to cost, and whether it should be paid for by superficial or by cubic feet. To this end a number of masons were imported and set to dress stones by daily labour, but they evidently knew what the object was, and got through as little work as they possibly could, breaking chisels in the most appalling manner. If hurried, and made to work hard, they took themselves off severely attacked by fever, or were urgently required at home on account of their mother's decease—that last resource of the native when he wishes to escape. Matters were complicated by the arrival of two or three native contractors wanting stone contracts. There is a brotherhood amongst stonemasons, a kind of trades union, and they stand by one another most loyally. It is so easy to hammer away at a stone for hours, and hardly make any impression. At last it became necessary to give out the work in contract, when the change became at once apparent, the chisels flew, the stones were turned out with amazing rapidity, the workmen ceased to get fever, and the mortality amongst their mothers ceased. Happy smiling faces greeted one instead of the woe-begone ones that used to lament their separation from home and friends whenever the sahib came near. The native is an adept in the art of deception.

Some stonework that required a little more thought in the dressing was that for the skewbacks for the splay arches of the new regulator, Fig. 51; it was thought that by having the skewbacks ready cut in stone, time would be saved in laying the stones, instead of having to cut bricks to the required shape in situ. Besides for the shorter abutments of the splay arches some additional strength would be given by having the arches at the joint with the abutment made of stone. As the native mason could not be expected to understand the drawings of the stones (Fig. 52), a model of the centering, and of the skewbacks, was made in mud. The masons had no difficulty in copying this, the accuracy of dimensions being insured by the use of templates.

Templates were employed to a very large extent in all the work upon the new dam and regulator. This was due to the influence of a very old master mason or "mistree," who had been employed upon the canal ever since its commencement. Most natives are careless, require constant directing, and are apt to think that they have no immediate responsibility in anything. They think that to advance their own views on any point will be considered an impertinence by the sahib. So they do slavishly what they are told, and when the result is failure say, "You told me to do so," or, "Your honour did not tell me to prevent such and

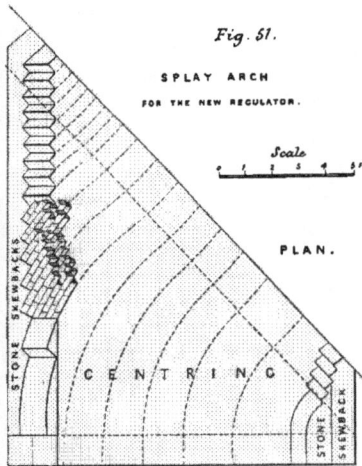

Fig. 51.

SPLAY ARCH
FOR THE NEW REGULATOR.

Scale

PLAN.

STONE SKEWBACKS

CENTRING

STONE SKEWBACK

Fig. 52.

BRICK ARCH

SECTION.

such a thing from being done." It was very different with old Kushial. He had his ideas as to how work should be done, and exceedingly sound ones they were. When told to do a thing he disapproved of, Kushial would listen patiently to the end, and say, "Very good, sahib;" then he would hang around for a bit, and would presently herald his objection (with his hands clasped in an attitude of the greatest reverence), with the remark, "Pardon my offence, your honour, but—" and then he would proceed to state his objections and explain how things should be done, and finish up by saying, "Of course your honour knows best, only I thought I ought to tell you what occurred to me." Of course Kushial was generally right, and his advice always listened to respectfully, if not always acted upon. He had not a particularly high opinion of the work of his fellow-countrymen, and would say of the masons, "What can be expected of such animals?" (Fig. 53). He carried his contempt for their understanding into the region of practical politics by making wooden templates for everything, no matter how simple, so that they should never have the chance of going wrong.

The heavy floor stones of the dam were laid by hand. Lifted by a crane in the stacking field on to a trolly, they were run down to the work, tipped off the trolly, and laid by hand. The men employed on moving and lifting stones are termed bundanis; they are fine strong men, and prefer to move and carry stones about by brute force, instead of using power of any kind. Where there is sufficient room to employ a number of men, this direct method of dealing with heavy weights is a very quick one. The harness they employ is so designed that every man must give an equal share of work; it is made for powers of two, four, eight, six-

Fig. 53.

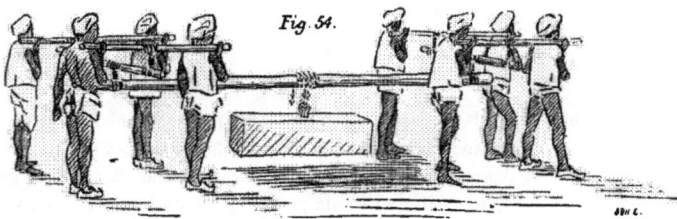

Fig. 54.

teen, or thirty-two men; there is nothing stiff about it, the poles being connected by ropes, so that the whole frame must be sufficiently supported at every point, i.e., if a man is unable to do his share of work, he will be forced down by the weight of his yoke (Fig. 54). The attachment to the stone being made by means of Lewis holes in the middle of the top there are no fastenings to interfere with the direct laying of the stones; when laid they are well bedded in mortar by repeated blows from a heavy mallet. A number of floor stones and those for the first courses of the piers were laid at night, but the cold in the bed of the river with the wind from the mountains blowing down the valley was very trying to the natives ; and the progress made at night was far from satisfactory, most of the bundanis' time being spent in crouching round the large fires provided for them. From these it was most difficult to drag them away. The scene—natives working by torchlight with the wild surroundings, and all the water about —is an exceedingly picturesque one. The bundanis chant verses and rhymes to keep themselves together when working hard. One man takes the principal part, and often indulges in compositions, when a good deal of abuse is heaped on the weight that is being moved, and the others all join in the refrain. The words of these songs will not, as a general rule, stand translating. The bundanis are a hard-working class of men, but even bundanis will shirk work occasionally. A young officer was putting up some temporary girders to replace a bridge that had been washed away. To hasten matters he ordered work to be carried on at night, and in order to see that there was no shirking, brought a small tent down to the work. For two nights he heard the bundanis chanting away at their work all night, but very little progress indeed was made. On the third night he appeared upon the scene without giving any warning, and found the bundanis seated comfortably round a fire, smoking pipes, and chanting with great zeal "Oh ! brother ; Oh ! brother ; pull together ; Oh ! brother."

A great deal of the engineer's time is taken up in circumventing the artifices of natives, for there are always a number who employ all their energies on trying to get as much pay for as little work as possible. It is customary in paying for earthwork to measure up the excavation pits after the earth has been removed, for the natives are unable to understand measurements made from plans or drawings. To enable measurements to be made accurately, every here and there pieces of the original soil are left untouched, and profiles are left between any two pieces of work. These are called "tatties." The native displays great skill in the selection of the positions of his tatties. He chooses the highest points, with loose soil on the top if possible, and then piling on as many inches as he can of earth to match, he leaves this to represent the depth dug. If there is a tuft of grass growing on the tattie, he will remove the top altogether and introduce a stratum of foreign soil. When earth is required for the embankments of irrigation channels, it is usually only stripped off the adjacent fields to the depth of 1 ft., so at to admit of the field being cultivated again. When the contractor is ordered to dig his borrow pits 1 ft. deep, he takes the most elaborate pains to dig only 6 in. or 8 in. and to make them appear of the full depth. He then expects the sahib to measure the superficial area of his excavations and assume them to be fully 1 ft. in depth.

The concrete in the foundations of the dam was put in by a number of petty contractors, for the exigencies of the work often required as much as possible to be poured on to one spot, so that it was impossible to keep the contractors' work separate. The quantity of ballast used was considered a good criterion of the amount of concrete put into the foundations. A stack of ballast on the Bailwalla Island was measured and made over to each contractor, his orders being to carry his ballast to the mixing floors himself. In a few hours there was enough ballast spilled between the stacks and the mixing floors to make a good metalled road, and each contractor was ready to swear that his men had spilled none of it! Then the ballast was measured on the mixing floors, and these being situated near the work, an eye could be kept upon them. Of course, in the hurry the contractor stacked the ballast so as to get as favourable a measurement as possible, and allowance had to be made for this. The Hindoo contractor can scarcely be inferior to the heathen Chinee in the depths of his cunning. Often his artifices are very transparent, but these obvious cheats are more often merely cloaks to cover some subtler villany.

The old works at Myapur are all built of boulder masonry plastered over. When plaster is used as a protection against weathering, and not merely to hide bad work, it is an admirable aid. The natives are famous for their plastering, and they are exceedingly fond of it. The shining white roofs of the Hindoo temples are all made of white plaster. A very handsome new temple has recently been built near Hurdwar; the roof was first made of sandstone, handsomely carved, and then coated with shining white plaster which for the time gave it the appearance of white marble. The strength of native plaster and the splendidly fine surface is obtained by beating it with wooden knives, by rendering the surface with finely ground lime with a trowel, and finally by polishing with pumice-stone.

TORRENTS.

For the greater part of its course the Ganges, after the manner of all Indian rivers, flows in a depression several miles in width. This low land in Northern India is called the " Khâdir." It consists for the most part of unculturable ground, but there is also a good deal of cultivation, and numerous hamlets are scattered about, and in places we come across fine old trees, showing that, although the course of the river is constantly shifting, cutting away old soil and depositing new, still the greater portion of the Khâdir has for many years suffered immunity from its insidious attacks.

Let us examine Khâdir at a spot where it is five or six miles in width, with the river running close under the left bank of the valley. The high bank of the valley is termed the " bhangar ; " it is, more often than not, sandy and cut up into ravines, clothed with scrub and jungle. Descending by one of these ravines we emerge upon the Khâdir of the Ganges (Fig. 55). Immediately beneath the bhangar the Khâdir is moist, the subsoil water from the high land oozes out of the soil, and although the ground has, for a short distance, an appreciable slope, it is often boggy and dangerous. This sloping ground leads to the Budhgunga, a deserted bed of the Ganges, now a long swampy depression running along under the right bank of the valley. It is filled for the most part with tall reeds and grass and abounds with dangerous quagmires, in which both elephants and horses have often disappeared, and in which numbers of cattle yearly meet their deaths. There is a story of an elephant that got bogged in one of these swamps; he sunk right away till nothing but the tip of his trunk remained above ground, and this continued moving for a couple of days after, showing that the poor beast was still alive ; a fearful death. Tigers, leopards, wild pigs, and the small hog-deer manage to shelter in these swamps, and as long as they keep to the larger ones are free from molestation, but the narrow swamps may be beaten for large game by dragging a long rope, the extremities of which are harnessed to elephants on opposite sides of the swamp. The elephants proceed along the edges and the rope flaps over the long grass between, making a rustling noise that frightens the wild animals much more than the ordinary beating of men or elephants, which they can understand, and causing them to break cover on either side.

Many parts of the Budhgunga consist of patches of deep open water forming lakes or lagoons. Although characterised by sticky bottoms the swamps may be crossed at many points, and most of these are marked by tracks, trodden down and free from jungle, for they are used by the herds of cattle that graze in the Khādir. Crossing the Budhgunga we find a belt of low sandhills running along its further edge, clothed with long grass and palm trees; and beyond stretches a sandy plain covered with coarse sikandar grass that grows in clumps, the spear-like stems of the flowers attaining a height of 15 ft. Crossing this we come to a patch of cultivation and a few old trees sheltering a hamlet, the inhabitants of which live mostly by cattle grazing.

Some of these Khādir villages shelter the most daring cattle lifters at the present time. A look-out is always kept up one of the tall trees, and should a stranger be descried making across the plain, any "foreign" cattle that may chance to be on hand are quickly driven off

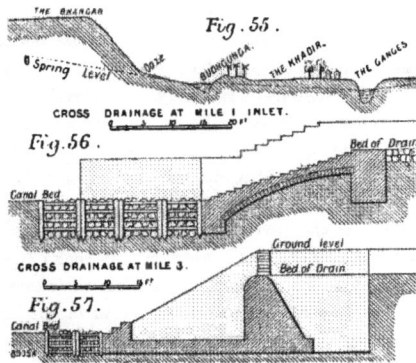

into safe hiding in the jungle, and the stranger finds the bland villagers engaged in the most peaceful and domestic occupations. These cattle lifters have adopted an admirable principle of small profits and quick returns that causes them quite to pose as benefactors to society, and keeps them out of the police courts. It is a cheap stolen beast supply association, in which the owner is given the first refusal of his own animal. Suppose a native clerk employed on the canal "loses" his pony; after some days fruitless search he will meet a villager who will tell him that another man has told him where the pony is to be found; this man, a stranger, on being introduced to the clerk, will tell him that if he chooses to pay him a quarter of the value of the pony he will take the money to the man who has "found" it and have the pony left at a certain place. This method of recovering a stolen animal is so satisfactory that the police officers are not informed of a tithe of the thefts that occur, and consequently the thieves enjoy considerable immunity from interference.

Beyond the village cultivation, we may cross a plain growing only a scanty crop of short grass and in some places quite bare; this ground is salty.

At last we arrive at the river itself, a vast sheet of shining white sand with the dry weather channel of the river flowing in the midst.

In taking a canal out of such a river, a spot would, of course, be chosen where the stream is near the bank of the valley on which it is intended to make the canal. The canal may then plunge boldly into the bhangar at once, and make towards the watershed of the country, or it may be taken along in the Khádir for some distance, in gradually increasing embankment, till it can be taken on to the bhangar nearly on a level with the ground surface. The former plan necessitates very heavy digging, the latter leaves the canal open to the danger of being some day attacked by the river floods and being much inconvenienced by the unstable nature of ground, soaked with the bhangar ooze. The Upper Ganges Canal is made on the former, the Lower Ganges Canal on the latter principle.

As a consequence of this alignment the Upper Ganges Canal starts off in heavy digging. It continues thus for the first twelve miles of its course, but this is rather from choice than necessity, for the slope of the country is so great in this portion near the hills that, were it not for other reasons, the canal bed might very quickly have been brought to nearly level with the ground, and the depth of digging reduced. In fact the aid of numerous falls has to be invoked in order to keep the bed at this depth. The most economical section for a canal being that in which the excavation is just sufficient to form the banks, there must be some very valid reason to account for this apparent extravagance. In fact the bed levels of the canal are determined by those of the principal torrents that have to be crossed before reaching the main watershed that divides the drainage of the Ganges and Jumna valleys.

These torrents are of two kinds : (1) Minor torrents, that only discharge such a volume that it may be allowed to enter the canal without fear of anything but a slightly increased volume that can be neutralised at the next escape. These, when they reach the canal, are provided with simple inlet falls to prevent their beds cutting back (Figs. 56 and 57). (2) Main torrents of such magnitude that provision must be made for their safe passage across the canal. In the case of the Ganges Canal these main torrents are four in number, and are named respectively, in the order in which they occur, the Rani Rao, the Puttri, the Ratmau, and the Solani (Fig. 58). All these have their source in the Siwalik range and are essentially torrents ; that is they only really run for a short time after rain has fallen in the hills, though the Ratmau and the Solani, having longer courses, partake more of the character of rivers and have generally a certain amount of water in them.

It has been previously stated that the disintegration of the Siwaliks is proceeding with great rapidity, and these torrents are the medium through which their disintegration takes place. Their courses wind right up into the heart of the range, and they bring down immense quantities of sand during every heavy rainfall. The Rani Rao and the Puttri lose themselves in the swamps of the Ganges Khádir, whilst the Ratmau is a tributary of the Solani which now flows into the Ganges, though formerly it flooded the Khádir much in the same way as the others.

These four torrents occurring in the first twenty miles of the course of the Ganges Canal afford excellent examples of the manner of disposing of such obstacles. The first two are carried over the canal, a super-passage, 300 ft. wide and 450 ft. long, being provided for each. The Ratmau is conveyed across by a level crossing, and the Solani passes under the canal, which crosses it upon the famous Solani Aqueduct.

Where they cross the canal the streams have the following characteristics : The Solani flows in a deep valley of its own, the Ratmau is embanked above the canal and has cut a deep channel for itself below, the Puttri is embanked both above and below its crossing, and the Rani Rao has a channel with fairly high banks. Speaking of the Puttri and Rani Rao, Sir Proby Cautley says, in his report, "the line of the Ganges Canal came in contact with these torrents high up in their courses and in the regions where, escaping from confined channels, they poured over the country broad sheets of sand." It was at first intended to keep the bed of the canal high, and take these torrents across in the same manner as the Ratmau, but the first flood that occurred after the excavation of the canal showed the futility of such an attempt, as the sand simply filled up the bed and obliterated the works. Cautley arrived at the following conclusions:

1. That it would be an evil of the first magnitude to let the torrents with their silt enter the canal.

2. That if a super-waterway be made of sufficient width there would be no wear and tear.

3. That there would be no retrogression of levels in the torrent beds, and that the torrents might be carried over the canal with perfect safety.

In order to carry out this programme, as he did not entertain the idea of syphoning the canal under the torrents, the necessity of keeping the canal in deep digging as stated above arose, though this evil was minimised as much as possible by having a fall immediately above each super-passage.

There has been no great difficulty experienced in dealing with these torrents except in the case of the Puttri, which has given some trouble, and only as recently as 1885 threatened to destroy the super-passage. Still they have to be closely watched and considerable sums of money spent yearly on training works to keep the torrents under proper control. Fig. 58 is a rough sketch or map of the torrents and their canal crossings; those of the Ratmau and the Solani work excellently. Considerable retrogression of levels has occurred in the Ratmau below the crossing. This cutting back of the bed is due in great part to the use that has been made of this channel as an escape for the canal. It has been checked by the introduction of cribwork weirs, filled with boulders, and faced with boulder masonry. The slope of the torrent before being interfered with was 8 ft. per mile, which is too great for any clear body of water running constantly. The silt brought down by these mountain torrents often counteracts the erosion due to their high velocity.

Fig. 59 is a sketch of the Ratmau crossing. Originally a dam was provided on the right bank of the canal, but being found unnecessary the piers have been removed, and the canal water is allowed to back up the torrent for some distance. During the rains a staff of some forty workmen is kept on this work, and on the appearance of a flood in the Ratmau, the escape dam gates are thrown open, and the regulator gates closed sufficiently to prevent the gauge in the canal below the regulator exceeding the maximum reading ordered to be maintained. There is a sharp bend in the canal just above the regulator, which is revetted on both sides, and these revetments, together with a bridge and the crossing works, form a very complete and extensive work. The Ratmau being embanked above the crossing, the drainage of the country about K is intercepted, and the water surface in the canal being too high to permit of its being disposed of by admission into the canal, it is brought under the flooring of the bridge (as shown by the dotted line), and dropped into the Ratmau below the escape dam.

K

The slope of the bed of the Rani Rao where it crosses the canal is 15 ft. per mile ; but as it only runs when laden with silt, this is not excessive. The floor of the super-passage is free from silt, and the bed has not suffered from erosion, a most satisfactory condition.

We now come to the consideration of the Puttri torrent and its crossing. The slope of the bed is about 25 ft. per mile, and in flood the torrent comes down 3 ft. or 4 ft. in mean depth, with waves 3 ft. or 4 ft. in height. The action on the bed is then tremendous, the whole sandy bed to the depth of several feet travelling with the torrent. With a stream of this kind it will be easily understood that a change of bed to the extent of several feet may occur in a single flood, and it will be hard to say what will be the condition of things after the lapse of several years. As during floods the bed is in motion to the depth of 2 ft. or 3 ft., it is evident that there ought always to be that depth of silt upon the super-passage in order to permit the flow of sand as well as water over it. It speaks volumes for the judgment of Sir Proby

Fig. 58.

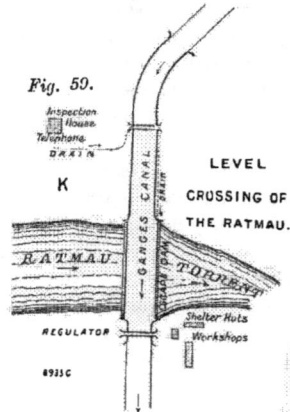

Fig. 59.

Cautley that there is about 5 ft. of silt upon the floor at the present day. Considering the data he had to go upon, it is wonderful that the regimen of the stream has been so well preserved.

Cautley said that the torrent here poured over the country in sheets of sand, that there would be no retrogression of levels, and that if the super-waterway were made sufficiently broad there would be no wear or tear on it. These conditions result naturally from the fact of the torrent having no free outfall. A few miles below the canal it ends in swamps and marshes ; there is no point where a retrogression can commence. Some day, when the torrent is connected with the Ganges, either directly or indirectly, retrogression of levels will commence, and will have to be dealt with. As long as there is silt on the floor of the super-waterway there can be no wear and tear on that structure. Nothing, however, seems to have been said about the tendency of the bed to rise ; such a contingency, in his estimation, could be easily met by raising the arches or making some other arrangement which might well be left to the intelligence of his successors.

When we take torrents "pouring over the country sheets of sand" and confine them within banks, it is difficult to judge exactly what will be the result of the operation. It would at first seem as if the confined floods should scour out a deep channel for themselves, but when we consider that the same quantity of sand that was formerly spread over a large area has now to be deposited within narrow limits, it seems as if the bed should rise. Floods of different duration, too, have quite different effects. A short heavy flood occurring when the hills are bare will bring down a lot of silt, and, spending itself before it reaches the end, will leave its sand to raise the bed. A long clean flood, on the other hand, when the hills are covered with verdure, will scour the bed and carry the silt right down to the swamps in the Ganges Valley.

Although a few feet more or less will make very little difference to the *régime* of the

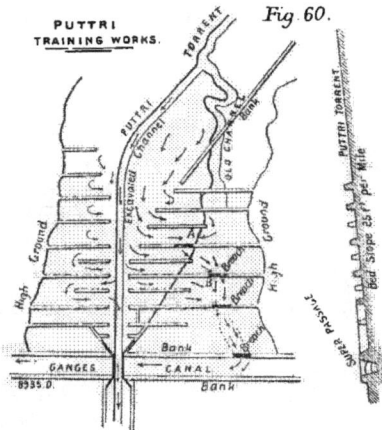

Fig 60.

torrent, it makes a considerable difference in its relations with the super-waterway, which is not constructed on the same scale as the Siwaliks and the Ganges Khādir. Something is being done towards reducing the detrition of the Siwaliks by the Forest Department in afforesting and protecting them against fire, but it is only the lower slopes that are so protected, and for many years yet a very great deal of silt must continue to be washed down, and it seems probable that the bed of the Puttri torrent must continue to rise.

Apparently the only permanent way of insuring the super-passage against a dangerous accumulation of silt is to have a free outfall for the torrent below it; either directly into the Ganges or into the Ratmau as shown in the dotted line *a b* (Fig. 58). The idea might for a moment present itself of diverting the Puttri into the Ratmau above the canal, and so abolish the super-passage altogether, but would be at once abandoned as only tending to reproduce the condition of things which existed when it was intended to take the Puttri across the canal by a level crossing. The project of taking the Puttri direct into the Ganges is an expensive one, whilst the authorities are exceedingly loth to introduce the stream with its immense quantities of silt into the Ratmau and Solani rivers, lest the spasmodic floods in these rivers should not be sufficiently strong to carry the sand away. With the Solani having no clear outfall, or only making its way to the Ganges through narrow artificial cuts, such a proceeding would be highly injudicious ; but giving the Solani flowing into the Ganges with a free outfall there seems to be nothing to hinder the Puttri being dropped into the Ratmau, as that river and the Solani can always be flushed with water from the canal. Meantime the danger of the obliteration of the super-passage by silt has been temporarily obviated by clearing the channel for some distance below the canal crossing.

The danger that threatened the canal in 1885 arose indirectly from the raising of the bed, but directly from the bursting of one apparently unimportant bank, through some unknown cause, possibly the creep of water through a rat-hole.

Fig. 60 shows the training works of the Puttri torrent above the super-passage. The long cross-banks tie on to high ground, and their ends towards the torrent are finished off by crib-

Fig. 61. CROSSING OF THE PUTTRI.

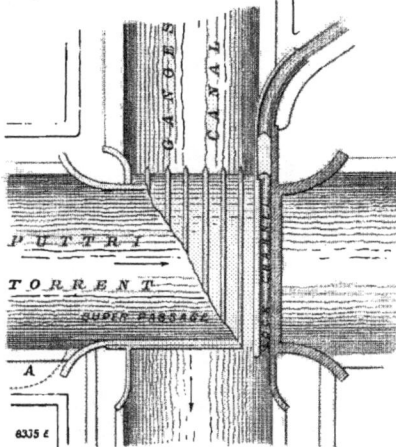

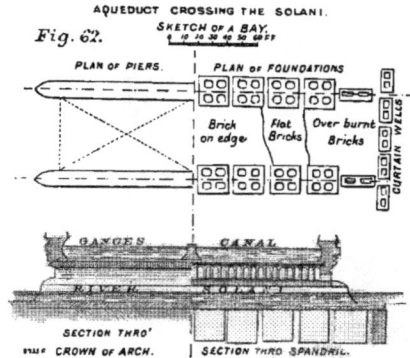

Fig. 62.

AQUEDUCT CROSSING THE SOLANI.
SKETCH OF A BAY.

work or masonry noses. They are at furlong intervals ; the top of each bank is quite level, and is about 6 ft. above the bed of the torrent opposite its nose. Consequently the crest of each bank is about 3 ft. higher than that of its next-door neighbour on the canal side. The short banks are to encourage the circulation of water with the object of depositing silt, and so making an unbreachable bank for the torrent. As long as the banks remained intact the water surface above each could only be connected directly with the water surface in the torrents one furlong above, but when a breach occurred at A the bank B became directly connected with the water surface two furlongs above itself, and in consequence had to take an additional 3 ft. of head, which topped it and caused a breach, and so with the next, the water finally topping the canal bank and making a large breach some distance above the super-passage. Fortunately the flood was of short duration, and the evil was repaired before the next.

The Puttri super-passage has a waterway for the torrent 296 ft. in width, and the work combines a fall and lock, which forms the entrance to the navigation channel, which above this fall is for some distance separate from the main canal on account of the rapid current, and the number of falls in the latter, Fig. 61. The super-passage is borne on arches, eight spans of 25 ft. each. In the flood of 1885 that caused the breach in the canal bank, the torrent was very near breaking into the canal close to the right upstream wing at A.

Fig. 62 is a sketch of a bay of the Solani crossing. The canal passes over this torrent on an aqueduct carried on arches, fifteen spans each of 50 ft. The canal waterway is 164 ft. in width and the depth upon the aqueduct about 10 ft. The foundations of this work are laid on blocks of wells sunk to a depth of over 20 ft. below the bed of the torrent. The Ratmau escape dam is also constructed on wells in a similar manner, as the softness of the soil is a source of great danger to any works exposed to any scouring action, whereas the foundations of the head-work at Myapur, where there is a hard shingle bottom, are comparatively shallow and made of solid concrete.

The Solani Aqueduct is an exceedingly handsome structure, and the view looking along the canal with its miles of revetted embankment is most imposing. A full description of the structure is to be found in Cautley's report on the "Ganges Canal," which is accompanied by an atlas giving large scale drawings of all the principal works on the canal as originally constructed.

RIVER TRAINING.

Owing to their unstable character, the torrents and rivers that come in contact with important engineering works in Upper India require careful training Not only is this the case where the works are of such a nature as to interfere with or alter their *régime*, as in the case of weirs or the heads of canals, but even when the works exercise no direct influence on the stream, as should be the case with large bridges and permanent quays, for the character of the banks is so unstable that the rivers, unless looked after, will often leave the works altogether.

The principal objects to be kept in view in controlling rivers and torrents are these :

1. Training with regard to permanency of direction, so that the works may not be out-flanked, or valuable land cut away.

2. Training with a view to maintaining the permanency of the bed slope.

3. Training to preserve an open channel amply sufficient to discharge the volume it is required to do.

4. Training to prevent or modify the evil effects of inundations in low-lying adjacent lands.

It might be supposed that with a lavish expenditure of money all these results could be insured by canalising the streams in question, but such is not the case, for with an Indian river there is always the possibility of the occurrence of a flood of such magnitude as to sweep away every bank and levée that may be raised to confine it within bounds. That the river floods have never exceeded a certain height within the memory of man is not a sufficient guarantee that no higher flood will occur. The collecting areas are very extensive, although it seldom happens that prolonged and heavy rain falls all over such areas at one time. Nevertheless, it is not a physical impossibility that at any time unprecedented rainfall may occur simultaneously over all the catchment areas of a river, causing an altogether unparalleled flood. Although we must not allow the fear of such a catastrophe to deter us from executing any necessary works, still the possibility of its occurrence should always be borne in mind, for we are often tempted to expend large sums on attempting to render permanent the *régime* of a river in the expectation that the irritating annual outlay on training and protective works may be done away with once and for all.

The object, in controlling a river, that must generally be borne in mind, as the word "training" implies, is to maintain the original characteristics of the river as unchanged as possible, and at the same time to keep such a check upon it as to prevent its breaking beyond certain limits. These limits will, however, only be defined in certain places where they are absolutely necessary. It would be manifestly absurd to undertake operations with the object of keeping a river in a certain course simply because it happens to run at present in that course, unless the advantages to be gained by such operations amply justified the expenditure incurred upon them.

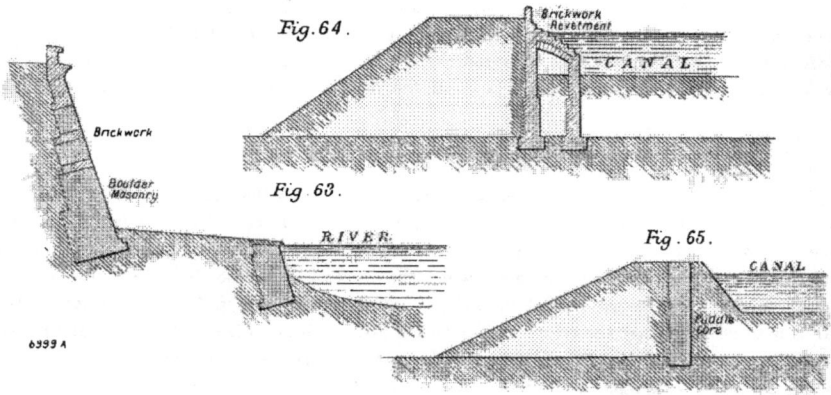

Fig. 64.

Fig 63.

Fig. 65.

The most permanent, but by far the most costly, means of insuring permanency of direction in a stream is by the employment of revetments made of masonry or of pitching, and with foundations of such a depth or aprons of such length as to secure them against destruction by undercutting. In Northern India these are only resorted to for short distances on account of the great expense they necessitate.

Perhaps the most economical and safest form of revetment is a combination of retaining wall and curtain used in the Fakirs revetment at Hurdwar and other places on the Ganges Canal, Fig. 63. The high retaining wall itself has comparatively shallow foundations, whilst the small curtain wall some distance in advance is the one that has to actually bear the brunt of the action of the river. Should this chance to fail at any point the injury may be repaired by temporary pitching, the main wall will remain uninjured, and it becomes unnecessary to take the heavy foundations very deep. Revetments are a good deal used on the Ganges Canal itself, but these are not always with a view to preserving the direction of the channel ; though such is the case in some instances, notably where the canal makes a sharp curve just above its crossing with the Ratmau Torrent. More often they are employed in heavy embankments, with a view to obviate the danger of a breach arising from any unsoundness of the earthen banks. The long embankment across the Solani Valley, and another, now abandoned, near the tail of the Etawah branch, are examples of the bold employment of revetment walls, Fig. 64. In the newer works of the Lower Ganges Canal, breaches in heavy embankments such as that across the valley of the Kali Nuddee are insured against by the presence of a core of puddled clay running like a wall through the centre of the bank, Fig. 65. This clay is stiff enough to resist the action of rushing water for a sufficiently long time to admit of a small breach, should it chance to occur, being closed.

Next to masonry revetments come marginal banks as a means of controlling the stream. These, though suitable for canals and sluggish streams, require in the case of rivers that run rapidly in flood, to be supplemented by spurs to prevent their being washed away by the scour of the river along their faces.

More usually employed in training works are spurs of considerable length run out from the natural high bank of the valley, or from an artificial bank made at such a distance from the river channel as to be safe from immediate danger of attack from the stream. These spurs are made of simple earth until they come within the action of the running water, when they are pitched with stone or protected by fascines or matting, and the actual nose, which is exposed to the direct attack of the river, is made of stone or concrete.

The reasons that make it desirable to train a river with respect to its direction are diverse. The Puttri Torrent, near the head of the Old Ganges Canal, requires training so that it may be led straight down upon the super-passage by which it crosses the canal. Near the head of the Lower Ganges Canal the River Ganges requires training both above and below the weir. Above, so that the main channel may be kept on the canal side of the river; and below, that it may be kept away from it.

This canal takes out of the Ganges at a point where the river commences to leave the right bank of the valley. Contrary to the plan adopted with the Upper Ganges Canal, which at once plunges into deep digging, the Lower Ganges Canal is taken as far as possible along the Khādir or low valley land. This arrangement effects a great saving in depth of excavation, but amongst other objections to it is the very serious one that the canal is never absolutely safe from the fear of destruction from the encroachments of the river, and the expense incurred in keeping the river away is considerable. Fig. 66 serves to show the necessity for training works and the general principles on which they are based. The sketch is supposed to be taken when the first and ninth miles of the canal are seriously threatened. But as the set of the river and the positions of the deep channels and banks vary from year to year, sometimes one point, sometimes another is attacked, and the character of the defensive works has to be varied accordingly. Wherever suitable channels occur, such as A, A, A, directing spurs are pushed out, increasing in length year by year, so as to induce the main stream to enter them and leave the right bank of the valley for good. Where there are no such channels we must be content with holding on to the ground that we have got, defending it from the action of the river by short spurs and lines of trees and branches placed along the banks B, B, and preventing any rush of flood water over it by cross-embankments C, C, C.

The large island above the weir (Fig. 67) divides the river into two main channels. The object of the works above the weir is to keep a good volume of water under the right bank in the channel A B, so as to prevent the formation of shallows obstructing the entrance to the canal. At the same time it is not desirable to close the channel C D altogether, for it is required to serve as an escape in heavy floods and prevent too great a strain being thrown on the channel A B and on the head works of the canal.

When the river is low and the drop gates of the weir are up between E and F, the only exit for the river is through the canal head G H, or by the under-sluices E G. This tends to keep the channel A B clear of silt. Spurs made of trees and branches placed across the entrance C D check the flow of water into that channel. The straight line marked on the island is the

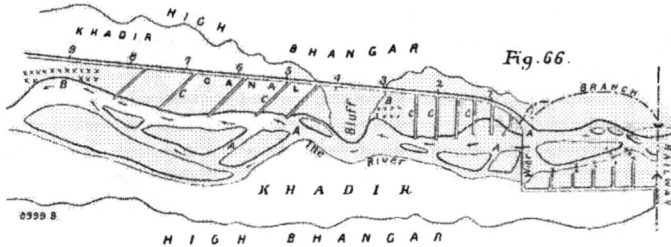

Fig. 66.

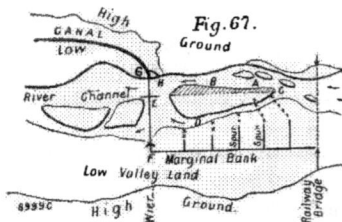

Fig. 67.

proposed left bank of the channel A B. There is no very urgent reason why it should be exactly where it is, but it is a good thing in works of this kind to lay down definite aims to be continually kept in view. This line being fixed upon as the bank of the channel, it is desirable to get rid of the portion shaded in the plan. The island is covered with a dense jungle of long grass and "jhow," which grows to considerable height and prevents heavy floods from flowing rapidly over the sandy soil. The clearance of jungle off the shaded portion is, therefore, a step towards its washing away, for should a heavy flood occur when this is bare, it will cut up the sandy surface into channels, and soon take it away altogether. The right bank of the channel is high ground, and is protected here and there to prevent the river encroaching. As the site of the canal head was probably shown at G H, mainly on account of the protection against out-flanking afforded by this high bank, it is a matter of the first importance to preserve it uninjured. A line should be laid down on this side also, and rigidly adhered to as the right boundary of the channel A B.

The left bank of the channel C D is low Khádir land of much the same character as the island. To prevent floods from spreading over this and out-flanking the weir at F, a large marginal bank has been constructed from J, the embankment of the Oudh and Rohilkund Railway to F, the left abutment of the weir; and at intervals along its face, cross-banks are run out towards the river, their noses protected by pitching or by trees and brushwood. The tree spurs at the entrance to the channel C D are carried right across the channel, and the left bank is protected by similar spurs, but these latter only extend a short distance beyond the bank into the channel. The trees are tied on to long ropes anchored down to crates filled with stones or block kunkur, Fig. 68. Those selected for this work must not be too large, as their transport across the heavy sand that forms the bed of the channel during the dry season would be very expensive; they should be as bushy as possible. The acacia (known as the babool tree in these parts) is suitable for the work. These tree spurs only last for one or two seasons, but no permanent arrangement can take their place, as changes are always occurring

Fig. 68.

in the river bed which can only be counteracted by a judicious arrangement of the tree spurs before the arrival of the next flood. As these spurs should not be constructed long before they are actually required, generally before the floods that occur in June, work on them has to be carried on during the hottest portion of the year. The glare from the water and from the sheets of white sand that form the beds of the dry channels is very great and trying to the eyesight.

Immediately below the weir, efforts are made to throw the deep channel of the river over to the left bank, see Fig. 66. Spurs made of kunkur are employed with this object; and lower down, tree spurs are used to a considerable extent.

Embankments of pure river sand serve very well to stop the flow of water across low ground, but when this material is employed for spurs projecting into the river bed they must be made exceedingly large and strong, and provided with permanent noses. They must also be protected against scour along their faces, even when there seems no immediate likelihood of such action taking place; small spurs run out at right angles, or a covering of grass matting, will insure this. Sand spurs, if required to last, must also be protected against the weather;

they are sometimes covered with a layer of good soil and turfed over, they then make almost sounder banks than those made throughout of strong earth, for animals do not burrow in the sand.

When, at any time, the river makes a set upon a bank which it is desirable to protect, and commences cutting away, it is exceedingly difficult to arrest the action. Hanging tree spurs may then be employed. Trees are anchored in lines to ropes upon the land, and as the ground cuts away the trees fall over with it and check the action of the current upon the bank.

Such training works are usually in the immediate charge of an upper subordinate, who lives on the spot, and they are superintended by the executive engineer of the canal, whose work often takes him to the other end of his division, a hundred miles away. As, during the hot weather, it is impossible to be out upon the burning sands during the heat of the day, the inspecting officer has to make his arrangements so as to see as much as possible every day in the shortest possible time. After a little experience he will discover the best method of inspecting his work so as to economise his time as much as possible. As an example of the kind of work that this inspection involves, let us follow the inspecting officer at Narora on one of his rounds. He proposes to start at daybreak to inspect the upper spurs above the weir. The previous evening he sends word to the petty contractors and foremen employed on the works he intends to visit, to warn them to be present at certain points the following morning. His boatmen are ordered to take a four-oared boat during the night up to the railway bridge at Rajghat, and a groom instructed to take a horse to the far side of the river, crossing by the ferry-boat below the weir, to there await his arrival at some convenient spot. The trollymen are told to have a trolly in readiness at Narora, to proceed to Rajghat by the branch line that was laid down at the time of the construction of the canal head and weir. Although the engineer starts at daybreak he will find that all his instructions have been faithfully carried out beforehand. His rifle and his note-book will be carried by the orderly who generally accompanies him on such expeditions, for trollying to Rajghat he may chance to come across a herd of antelopes with a good black buck amongst them, out feeding in the cool of the morning. At Rajghat he leaves his trolly and takes to the boat with its crew of sturdy Hindoos, rowing in excellent time with a form that is a compromise between English sea and river rowing. They have the landsman's long swing and straight back, but finish the stroke with the sailor's jerk. One or two stray alligators may be passed lying upon the sandbanks in the river, but it is later in the heat of the day that they come out in numbers to bask on the warm sand. They lie close to the water's edge, their noses to the river ready to rush in at the slightest alarm. The glare of the early sun off the water is most trying, but the head of the channel C D is soon reached. As this channel is probably dry, the officer will have to abandon the boat and order the boatmen to return to Narora. After plodding through the heavy sand on foot, counting trees and measuring work (see Fig. 68), he arrives at the spot on firm ground where his horse awaits him, and rides down the marginal embankment to the weir. Giving the horse to one of the watchmen, he may walk home across the weir to his bungalow, distant about three-quarters of a mile.

The works below the weir are more easily inspected, as a trap can be sent several miles down the canal bank, and there will only be a short walk from the boat to the canal across the green Khádir. Such is an example of the outdoor inspection work that the officer in charge of river training work does, day by day, during the hot season. There is a considerable monotony about the scenery, and there is no society, as there are no other European inhabitants at Narora, but the work is very interesting, and plenty of office work keeps him employed during the daytime.

Were the Narora weir built of masonry of the full height required to give a full supply in the canal, it would unduly interfere with the bed slope of the river; but the masonry crest is kept low and the extra height obtained by falling gates which are let down in floods. Even as it is, there is a tendency to the formation of sandbanks above the weir. Unless weirs are very carefully constructed, this always occurs, and a large island forms above the weir, rendering the greater part of the crest practically useless, and throwing an undue volume upon the exposed portions.

Beyond keeping the weir low no training works are undertaken at Narora for the preservation of the bed slope of the river. It has been mentioned above that this kind of training divides itself into two heads, to prevent the cutting back of the bed where the slope is excessive, and to give increased slope where it is insufficient. The former result is usually obtained by introducing bars or weirs into the bed and so reducing the slope between them. Such a method is adopted with the Ratmau Torrent as described in the last article, and in the Old Ganges Canal some distance below Roorkee, where the canal runs through soft sandy soil in deep digging, a number of bars known as the Damāt bars are introduced, made of crates filled with boulders. They are sufficiently close together to make a practically continuous bed slope, and they act more as bed forms than as weirs. Still the velocity is considerably accelerated over each, and they form rather an impediment to navigation. Another method of attaining the same end is to render the channel less direct, so that in travelling from point to point the fall will be less sudden; this is sometimes done with small drainage lines that threaten to cut back and assume large proportions. The drainage may be made to circulate amongst banks instead of flowing straight.

Questions three and four, training to preserve an open channel, and to modify the evil effects of inundations, belong more correctly to the subject of drainage, and will be dealt with under that head.

DRAINAGE.

In our last article attention was given to measures undertaken in order to train a river so as to protect important works from injury, owing either to a change of direction or to the cutting back of the river bed. We now come to the consideration of the case where it is deemed advisable to increase the discharging capacity of a channel. For instance, when extra drainage or escape water from canals is introduced into comparatively small rivers, it is sometimes advisable to take steps to enable the river channel to meet the extra tax upon its carrying power. It then becomes either necessary to enlarge the section, or to increase the bed slope of the channel. The latter object is generally comparatively easy of attainment in Northern India, as the small rivers have very winding channels caused by such opposition in the soft soil of the valley as they meet with from beds of stiff clay, or deposits of kunkur.

It is a simple process to cut through the necks and shorten the course of the stream. Fig. 69 (page 76) indicates the lines such cuts would take. Often an old and more direct bed of the river will be found on the far side of the valley, and it may sometimes be expedient to train the river into this. Care must be taken in undertaking operations of this description to commence low down the river, for if straightened in the upper parts of its course, this portion will discharge more rapidly than the lower reaches, which will in consequence be badly flooded. The sharp bends in the rivers of the Do-āb are mostly of the character shown in Fig. 70. In this sketch the left bank in the section is of clay, but it is gradually being cut away, whilst the right bank as gradually encroaches. In this manner a stream of this kind is for ever changing its course ; slowly, it is true, until during a heavy flood, the neck A B bursts suddenly. The channel C D will then be left a backwater, and in time filled up with fine clay. The section shows the manner in which the vegetable soil gradually covers the sandy bottom of the Khādir. As the sandy pit rises above the water surface, it soon covers itself with a coarse jungle growth of "jhow," which, when the river is in moderate flood, collects the lighter particles of earth and so rises until the sand has a good covering of cultivable soil. Sometimes a very heavy flood

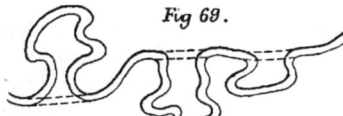

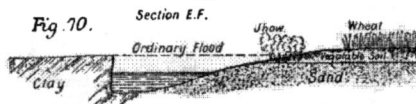

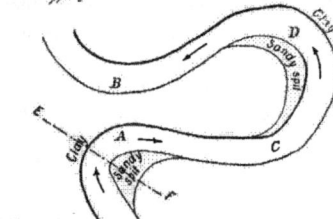

Fig 69.

Fig. 70.

Section E.F.

Fig. 73.

will break through a number of necks and straighten the channel considerably. Such was the case in the Kali Nadi in 1884 and 1885, when two heavy floods completely altered the channel of the stream. After the floods the course was materially straightened, the bed was scoured out deeper and wider, and the weeds which had threatened to completely choke the channel, entirely swept away. This was most opportune, as a project had some years previously been drawn up for the straightening of the lower reaches of this river, but was not carried out, mainly on account of its great cost. The second of these floods, which occurred in June, 1885,

FIG. 71.

was much greater than that which took place in October, 1884. It was altogether unprecedented, as was shown by the fact that the valley of the river was not sufficiently large to carry it comfortably. In the narrow gorges the banks were cut away into cliffs, and numbers of villages were swept away or reduced to ruins, and all the bridges across the stream destroyed (see Fig. 71, page 77). The cause of this disastrous flood was a rainfall of 16 in. occurring in one day all over the northern portions of the catchment area, and this at the commencement of the rains, when the ground was bare after the summer drought, and there was almost no vegetation to arrest the sudden discharge of rain water into the river.

River training, to obtain a larger section, often takes the form of straightening the channel and allowing the increased velocity to scour it out, but sometimes actual clearance by manual labour is resorted to.

The Puttri Torrent, below the canal crossing, is an example of this; it has recently been silt cleared quite after the manner of a canal, the sand being dug out and carried to the sides by hand.

Fig. 72.

The Solani River is an example of the necessity of providing a clear channel where practically none existed before. This river, which had no clear outfall into the Ganges, used to come down during the rainy season and, meandering through a series of swamps, flood the whole Ganges Khādir. This want of outfall to the swamps kept the Khādir in an unculturable condition, the greater portion being covered with dense grass jungle, only negotiable on an elephant, and sometimes quite impracticable owing to quagmires and quicksands. Still, during the dry season most of the land was utilised for feeding cattle, and the annual flooding did not interfere with them, for during the rainy season this portion of the Khādir was abandoned by the cattle grazers. But with the introduction of the escape from the Ganges Canal *via* the Ratmau Torrent it sometimes happened that a large volume of water had to be poured into the Khādir at a time when the cattle grazing season was at its height; and it became necessary to open out a through channel for the Solani into the Ganges. This has now been practically accomplished, and with very little expenditure. The principal obstruction to the flow of the river was offered by extensive flat beds of hard clay. Shallow channels were cut into these in the hope that the river being given a lead, would be able to cut its way through; but the clay was too stiff to permit of this. By sinking wells along the course of the river the clay was ascertained to be of no great depth. Narrow cuts were then made right through the beds with excellent effect. The river floods rushing through the narrow channels, scoured away the sand beneath and undercut the clay, which fell in large lumps, forming eventually a fairly broad channel (Fig. 73).

An object often aimed at in river training is to protect low-lying culturable tracts in the valley from swamping and valuable land from being cut away by the formation of new channels. These ends, though practically accomplished by the enlargement and straightening of the dry weather channel, are more directly attained by protective embankments or levées. In the project mentioned above for the improvement of the Kali Nadi was included an extensive

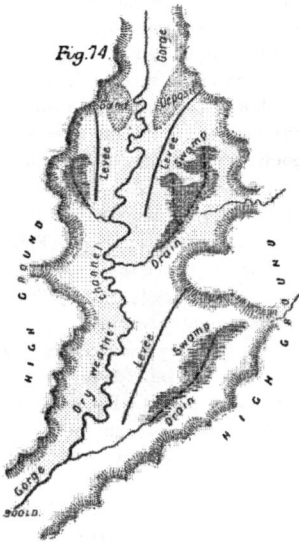

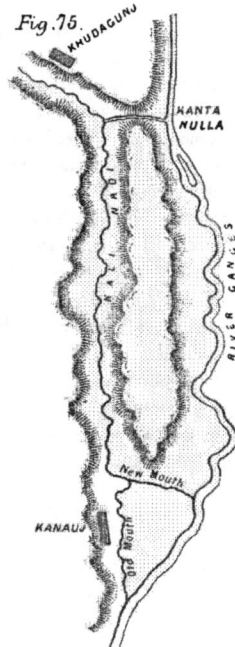

Fig.74

Fig.75

system of levées and drains for the protection and improvement of the valley lands, a considerable portion of which are low and swampy, Fig. 74. The levées were designed to prevent the river spilling into the upper portions of the swamps, and each of these was to be provided with a drain having its exit at the lower end. The slope of the valley is sufficient to prevent the river from backing far up these drains. As a considerable amount of irrigation is done from the river water, it was proposed to let earthen pipes into the levées, so as to admit of the continuance of irrigation. It is just as well that this project was never carried out, as the great flood of 1885 would have swept away every bank and filled up most of the drains with sand. In the flood years 1884 and 1885 the swamping of the valley, which was considerable, was not due so much to the heavy floods in the river, the effects of which quickly passed off, as to the percolation water from the high ground on either side. In many places the water was oozing out of these banks considerably above the level of the valley, and against this the levées would be absolutely no protection, and the drains would only slightly mitigate the evil. The actual direct effects of the floods were in themselves sufficiently disastrous without this trouble being piled on the cultivators of the valley. Whole tracts were covered with deposits of coarse unculturable sand, and the flat Khādirs ploughed into deep furrows and channels, quite destroying the irrigating watercourses and rendering their restoration a difficult and expensive undertaking. Fortunately most of the villages that cultivate the valley also possess lands upon the high ground, so that there was very little absolute destitution.

The action of the flood was instructive. Where it rushed through the narrow reaches of the valley with great velocity the channel was scoured out to several hundred feet in width and far below its normal depth, but where the flood flowed through the broader portions the dry weather channel was not much altered, but the broad Khādir was furrowed and cut about. The deposits of heavy sand took place at the points where the floods emerged from the narrow gorges into the broader valley.

The object in training the Kali Nadi being to obtain a more rapid discharge, the outfall into the Ganges required attention. This outfall is somewhat peculiar (Fig. 75). The mouth proper of the river is close to the sacred city of Kanauj, under the walls of which its channel runs. When Kanauj was a flourishing city the Ganges flowed close by, but gradually it has worked away, the piece of valley A B has been formed, and Kanauj has lost a good deal of its sanctity as a bathing place. It is said that in order to bring the Ganges water past Kanauj again, a cut was made some thirty miles higher up the stream, where the Kali Nadi and the Ganges run very close to one another. This cut is known as the Kanta Nulla.

As a general rule a little water from the Kali spills through this into the Ganges, but when the latter is in flood its water backs up through the Kanta Nulla, and flows down the valley of the Kali to Kanauj.

The whole character of the Kali Nadi valley below the junction with the Kanta Nulla is different from what it is above, the Khādir being composed of coarse rough sand more like the Ganges than the Kali Nadi valley formation. It was feared lest this deposit of Ganges silt in the lower reaches of the Kali Nadi might obstruct that river and eventually close the Kanauj mouth ; so, some years ago, the Kanta Nulla was closed by a high bank and the valley of the Kali, and the Ganges once more divided. This bank was topped and carried away by the flood of 1885, and there appears to be no adequate reason why it should at present be restored. There is very little danger that the Ganges silt will obstruct the flow of the Kali towards Kanauj, for it has already attained to as great a height as it is capable of doing. The Ganges cannot go on piling up silt to an indefinite height. This silting up seems to indicate that the Ganges has no tendency to burst through the Kali Nadi and make a channel for itself to Kanauj. Again, the fact that the Kali and Ganges are usually in flood at the same time prevents any sudden fall from the former into the latter river from causing a cutting back and deepening of the Kanta Nulla sufficiently to form it into a permanent mouth of the Kali.

In the flood of 1885 the Kali Nadi cut a new outlet into the Ganges a few miles above Kanauj by the channel C D, Fig. 74, so that the once famous city of Kanauj, now little more than a great collection of ruined temples, is deserted by both the Ganges and the Kali. As A B may be looked upon as a delta of the Kali, this change can do no harm to the river above; it is only Kanauj that suffers.

This glimpse into the condition of the Kali Nadi serves to demonstrate the danger which was pointed out in a previous article of attempting the canalization of the Indian rivers, without the very gravest examination and experiment. It is a question whether the soil of most swamps is sufficiently productive to repay a very heavy outlay on their reclamation. Experiments have been conducted on a small scale, and the Chaumaji Swamp in the Mainpuri district is a specimen. Some of the land which produces good grass when soppy and under water, as soon as it is drained bursts into a salty efflorescence, and when cultivated is only capable of producing a stunted blade of wheat here and there. Again, it is little use taking any measures to drain the swamps unless of such a nature as to ensure continuity, for if allowed to go out of cultivation for a single year, a crop of coarse deep-rooted grass and weeds springs up, which is exceedingly difficult to eradicate.

A considerable area of these swamps is covered with a layer of stiff clay, which, when kept thoroughly wet, will grow grass and sometimes rice, but if drained and allowed to dry and cake, even grass roots are unable to penetrate, and cultivation is out of the question.

It appears from the above considerations that the principles laid down for river training works, namely, that nature should be assisted, and no wholesale attempts at reform made, should be also applied to the case of the drainage of these swamps. The natural drainage lines (and there is a stream more or less defined running out of every hollow, Fig. 73), should be cleared out, so that the water level in the swamp, and consequently the wet area, may be reduced; but it seems impolitic to attempt to reduce lands, placed by nature in low moist situations, to the same condition as those which are situated high above the spring level of the country.

We would here put in a plea for the ducks and snipe, and the sportsmen thrown out of employment by all these drainage operations. Whilst at home societies are formed for the protection of common land, and recreation grounds are being thrown open in every direction (a certain amount of amusement being admitted to be not only beneficial but necessary to keep the human race in a good state of health), we, in India, are steadily encroaching on the only playgrounds that make life endurable to numbers of Englishmen. How dreary will be the existence of thousands of officers, civil and military, scattered all over the country, often in isolated situations, cut off from all society, when they are deprived of their only amusements, shooting and hunting. It is not only to the Europeans that this applies. The wild fowl that every cold weather put in an appearance on the plains of Northern India, contribute very materially towards the support of the population; and the natives are not so pampered that we need deprive those amongst them whose religion permits them to eat meat (including all the Mahommedans and a large percentage of the Hindoos) of any dainty that Providence has sent to gladden their miserable lives. Countless numbers of teal are yearly netted and eaten by the natives. It may be opposed that even after these drainage works are carried out there will still remain extensive swamps undrained for the ducks and snipe to take to. This, if true as far as the birds are concerned, is but poor consolation for the villagers, who can scarcely go

F

hundreds of miles to trap them, or to the sportsman who wants a day's recreation near his station or cantonment.

Although it seems advisable to let natural swamps take care of themselves, the formation of new ones by waste from our irrigation works must be carefully guarded against. The banks of the Lower Ganges Canal, running as it does for many miles close under the bhangar edge in the Ganges Khādir, obstruct the flow of the surface drainage, and the creation of swamps on the right bank of the canal would be the result were not proper arrangements made for their drainage. Syphons are provided under the canal at several points and a deep drain running parallel to and close under the bank is fed by numerous smaller channels, and keeps the swamps sufficiently dry for the cultivation of rice and sugar-cane.

On the left bank the percolation from the canal is provided for by a drain which is eventually led off to the Ganges. Keeping these drains clear of silt and weeds involves a great deal of expense and trouble, but the better the condition in which they are kept the less trouble they give. If allowed to get out of order for a short time, clearance becomes immensely difficult on account of the depth of water.

It is not only in the low-lying Khādir lands that the question of providing for the drainage of percolation water arises. All over the Do-āb are hollows and depressions, and these it is not always possible for the line of canal to avoid. Wherever a canal passes through or close to one of these depressions steps must be taken to prevent its becoming swamped and water-logged.

The tract of country between the Kali Nadi and the Ganges, irrigated by the Fategarh branch of the Lower Ganges Canal, affords a very striking example of a complication of drainage depressions, which it is impossible to avoid altogether, whatever care we may expend upon the selection of a line. These depressions are old river channels, and as they wind in every direction it is most difficult to make arrangements for draining them. Fig. 76 is a rough sketch of a piece of this system, the arrows showing the direction in which the water flows when it is sufficiently deep to do so.

The windings are generally channels 200 ft. or 300 ft. in width, and in heavy rainfall 3 ft. or 4 ft. deep, with a very sluggish current. They dry up soon after the rains, and various crops of wheat, barley, sugar-cane, or rice are grown in them, according to their depth and the amount of moisture or wet that they contain. One wet year is not generally sufficient to cause the water to flow, but after two or three in succession they turn into lakes and sluggish rivers. The depressions on the right bank of the Fategarh branch have been drained for the last thirty miles in order to permit of canal water being escaped into them, but all the upper portion, covering a tract of country about 50 miles long by 20 wide, is still untouched, and it is a difficult question to decide whether drainage schemes should be undertaken or not. The country presents a vastly different appearance in different years. The ordinary aspect of the piece of country depicted in Fig. 76 is that of an extensive sandy plain in which the canal distributaries are laid out in apparently fantastic curves. If we ride along any of these distributaries, however, the varying height of the banks above the ground surface and the occasional appearance of a syphon will show that the distributaries occasionally cross drainage depressions whose courses, indicated here and there by crops of sugar and rice, necessitate the alignment. It is quite impossible, however, to tell by eye the direction in which drainage water would flow in these hollows. The remainder of the plain grows a good crop of indigo in the hot weather, and a poor one of wheat in the cold season. After a succession of wet years, such as '84, '85, and '86, the place presents a very different aspect. During the continuance of the rains the depressions are turned into broad sluggish rivers, the fields are sodden, and the indigo is so stunted and brown as not to be worth the cutting ; whilst after six months of dry weather the depressions are swampy marshes, and the indigo is replaced by coarse grass and weeds which are exceedingly hard to eradicate. The soil being very sandy, this unfortunate tract of country is always in extremes. During dry years the inhabitants appeal piteously for canal irrigation, the nature of the soil precluding the construction of stable wells ; in wet years they cry out for drainage. For a few years after the introduction of the Fategarh branch, there was universal satisfaction, indigo cultivation was eagerly taken up, and many factories established. Then came the wet seasons indicated above with the spongy soil soaked

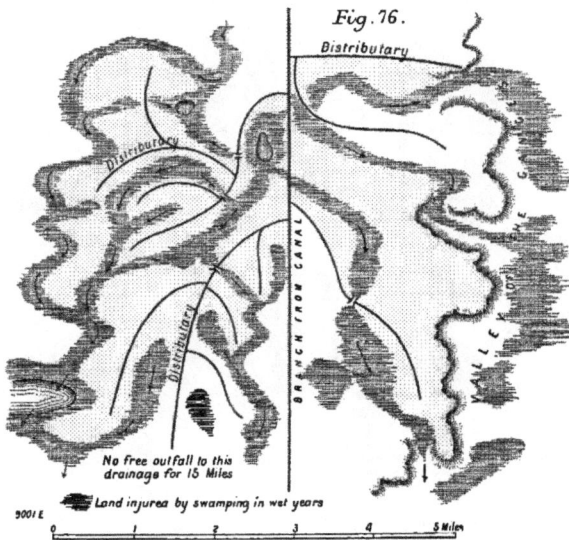

Fig. 76.

Distributary

No free outfall to this drainage for 15 Miles

Land injured by swamping in wet years

9001 E

0   1   2   3   4   5 Miles

to saturation, and the demand now is for drainage instead of irrigation. Were drainage schemes undertaken and no water permitted to rest in the hollows, it is more than probable that in a year or two there would be a great outcry that " the Government has run off all our rain water in order to drive us to take canal water for our rice and sugar-cane." When once we commence to interfere with the agricultural arrangements of a tract of country, there is no knowing how far the interference will have to be carried, and we must be prepared to bear abuse for every ill that happens, whether it is the fault of the season or of the idle cultivators themselves.

There is no place near at hand into which the tract of country (Fig 76) could be directly drained. On one side are the windings of the Baghar and on the other the Khādir of the

Ganges, both so swamped already that the inhabitants would cry out lustily were any attempt made to make them the receptacle of other people's superfluous drainage water. It seems probable, however, that in the end a comprehensive drainage scheme will have to be undertaken for this piece of country. As the tracts irrigated from wells are few in these parts, the well irrigation can be replaced by that from the canal distributaries in the event of the wells running dry, as they will probably do on account of the draining of their supply reservoirs. If it is ascertained after the experience of a few dry seasons that the land does not return to its normal

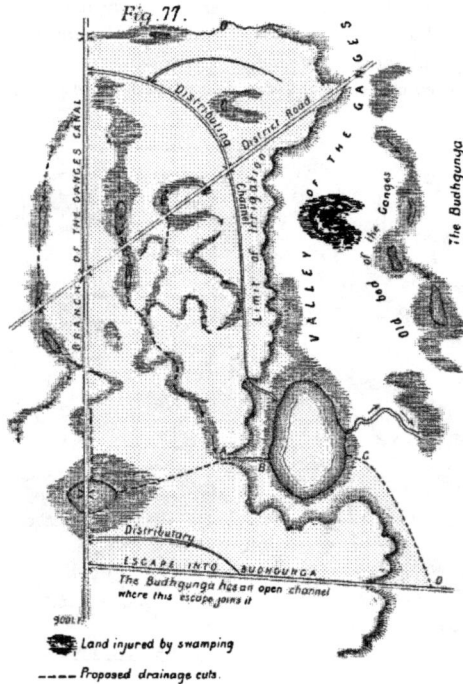

Fig. 77.

Land injured by swamping

Proposed drainage cuts.

condition, but still remains more or less soppy, it will be incumbent on the irrigation department to undertake a sufficient drainage scheme.

Fig. 77 is a sketch of a piece of ground higher up the Fategarh branch, which is susceptible of comparatively easy drainage through a well defined ravine A B leading into a large swamp in the Ganges Kādir, and thence by a channel which would require some clearing into the Budhgunga or else into the escape by C D. The Budhgunga, however, at this point is in much the same condition as the River Solani mentioned above, with no free outfall into the Ganges. The dotted lines show the direction the drainage cuts would take. The natives have very peculiar ideas about drainage. For instance, they attributed the swamping of the land C to the presence of the new metalled road D E, which is amply provided with drainage culverts.

When asked to explain how they knew that this road arrested the flow of water, they replied that the water was not running through the culverts at all, but stood at the same level on both sides of the road, which clearly showed them to be too small : " Make them twice as large and then water will flow through ! " The sugar and rice in the Budhgunga is often swamped by the percolation from the high ground, and it is possible that some day a scheme for its partial drainage will be undertaken. A long embankment has already been placed across the head of this depression by the Canal Department to prevent the Ganges floods entering it. Of course works of this kind ought to be undertaken by the villagers themselves, but these swamps are so long and pass through such a number of villages, many of them suffering from the sorest poverty, that it is almost impossible to obtain that universal co-operation without which any local attempts at improvement would only end in failure.

IRRIGATING CHANNELS.

The essential features of an irrigation scheme are the earthen channels in which the water is conveyed over the surface of the country ; the masonry works by which they are carried across drainage depressions ; and the head works by which a constant and regular supply of water is secured.

The considerations to be weighed in selecting a site and designing the details of head works and the main points to be looked into in crossing drainage lines have been discussed in previous articles. In the present it is proposed to consider, in the same practical spirit, some details of the distributing channels themselves ; details which, at first sight, may seem almost beneath the attention of scientific engineers, and which young and inexperienced officers are apt to stigmatise as "mud scraping," but which make all the difference between a successful and reliable system that will work smoothly in seasons of excessive demand, and one by which only a precarious supply can be assured, through the anxious exertions of individual officers, at seasons when their energies are already taxed to their utmost.

In the present series only the points absolutely essential to the success of an irrigation project have been dealt with ; such matters as bridges, locks, plantations, canal roadways, and inspection houses, although their inspection and maintenance take up a very great portion of the agricultural engineer's time and energies, and conduce most materially to the smooth working and financial successes of the system, are yet only accessories ; very important ones it is true, but still accessories in which a great deal of latitude may be left to individual taste.

The data required before an earthen water channel can be designed are :

1. The alignment of the channel.

2. The levels of the bed and water surface relatively to the ground levels.

3. The volume of water required.

The question of alignment so as to obtain the best command of the country as economically as possible without interfering with existing drainage was discussed in Art. IV. of this series.

In determining the levels or bed slope and the cross-section of the channel the following points should be borne in mind :

a. The fall of the ground surface will decide whether a continuous slope can be given, or whether the channel is to be divided into a number of reaches connected by falls or weirs.

b. The character of the soil will dictate the maximum velocity that may be given to the current without causing erosion of the bed and banks.

c. The character of the source whence the supply of water is drawn will determine the minimum velocity that must be maintained. Water heavily laden with salt will require a steep slope to keep a clear channel, as will water in which weeds flourish in profusion.

d. The depth of water, and consequently the cross-section of the channel, will considerably influence the slope of the bed; in fact, the section and the slope can only be decided upon with reference to one another, both depending on the volume to be discharged or the area to be irrigated.

e. For purposes of navigation it is advisable to keep the current as slow as possible, but

f. For economical reasons it is best to give a steep slope so as to reduce the magnitude and number of the falls and locks.

In starting new canals where there has previously been no experience of the kind, it is at first impossible to reconcile these conflicting interests, for the water on entering the canal will not necessarily behave in the same manner as it did in its savage condition. In the great rivers the bed is generally composed of coarse sand, unfavourable to the growth of weeds, and it is annually scrubbed and cleaned out by rapid floods laden with sand. In the canal the weeds have a bed of good productive soil on which to flourish, and an almost constant depth of water, just suitable to maintain them in a healthy condition.

The water on which the canals of the North-West Provinces depend for their supply, that of the rivers Ganges and Jumna, varies in character with the different seasons of the year. During the winter months, when the rivers are low, it is beautifully clear and transparent. In the spring, when the snow commences to melt, it grows turgid and milky, but does not carry a great amount of sand ; but, at the commencement of the rains in June, the water becomes thick with silt, and in heavy floods is as thick as peasoup and has a powerful and unpleasant odour. This is, of course, the season when there is least demand for irrigation, and sometimes the demand ceases entirely throughout the rains, so that the canals can be laid dry and the silt-laden water excluded. This would prevent, to a great extent, the channels getting choked with silt deposits, but there are also reasons which make the introduction of silt-laden water desirable. Were the cross-sections and bed slopes of all the channels in a canal system so proportioned that the velocity would be sufficient to carry the silt right on until it is finally spread over the irrigated fields, the benefit derived from the land from its fertilising influence would be considerable.

Again, it has been found that water weeds, like all other plants, require plenty of light for their development, and the thick flood waters kill them down more successfully than any other method. A deposit of fine silt on the bed and banks of the channels render them watertight, and thus save an immense deal of waste from percolation.

In places where the channel passes through rotten or porous soils, this percolation reaches its maximum, and besides the waste entailed, disastrous breaches are necessarily of frequent occurrence. In such places it is advisable to incur the extra expense of constructing double banks. In the tanks left between them a deposit of silt is encouraged until eventually they are entirely filled up with good soil ; when they may be cultivated or turned into plantations (Figs. 78 to 81). All fear of breaching is then removed and valuable oases established in the barren plains, for these or sandy rotten soils are for the most part unproductive. The upper ends of these silt traps soon fill up, and it is only by keeping a clear channel through the deposit that the whole tank can be properly silted up.

The ideal channel would be one so constructed that the bed and banks would collect a sufficient coating of fine silt to render them impervious to percolation. When this condition has been reached the silt deposit should cease, any further action in this direction merely tending to reduce the section. It is almost impossible to design a channel straight off, that will fulfil these conditions, but much may be accomplished by keeping them in view from the very outset.

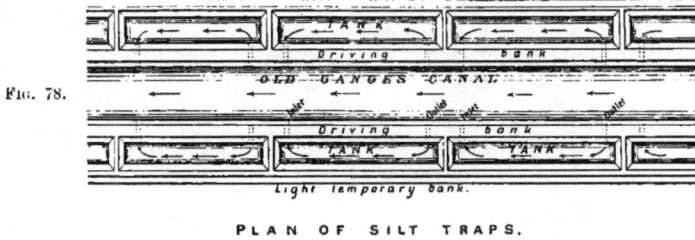

FIG. 78.

FIG. 80.

PLAN OF SILT TRAPS.

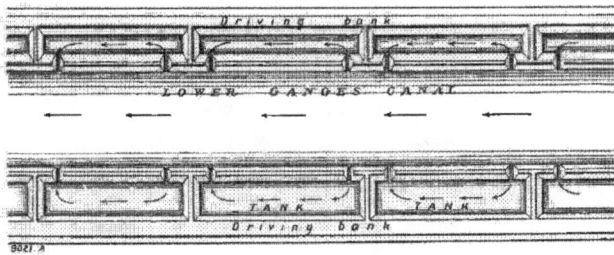

FIG. 79.

FIG. 81.

Thus, it will generally be advisable to design the channel of larger section than the one theoretically required, and where the slope of the country will lend itself to such a design, to make the bed slopes less steep than calculated. Of course, where the slope of the country is so slight (a rare occurrence) as to preclude the necessity of introducing artificial falls, this last is difficult of accomplishment, but, given a good slope to the country, and, as a consequence, a channel designed in a series of reaches connected by falls, the attainment of this end is comparatively easy.

We assume that the theoretical cross-section and bed slope are sunk so as to give a sufficient velocity to the water, to sweep along all the silt with which it is ever laden. It may be found that this velocity is so great as to cause erosion of the bed and banks and so destroy our slope and section at the same time. By making our cross-section larger, and the bed slope in each reach less steep than those indicated by theory, the current will travel with considerably reduced velocity and a deposit of silt will result. The deposit on the bed of the channel will be more pronounced towards the head of each reach, and there will be a gradually decreasing deposit towards the tail, until a bed slope has become established, which is sufficiently close to the theoretical one to institute a condition of permanent régime, with no tendency to cut away or to accumulate further deposits. The cross-section, also, narrows first at the upper end of the reach. When this portion has become narrow enough to sufficiently increase the velocity the accumulation practically ceases, and the silt is shot past to be deposited lower down. The silting up of the bed and banks of the channel thus proceeds until the whole reach has attained the desirable condition of permanency.

The enlargement of the section and reduction of the bed slope, must not in the first instance be too exaggerated, or it will lead to the precipitation of the heavier coarser silt, the

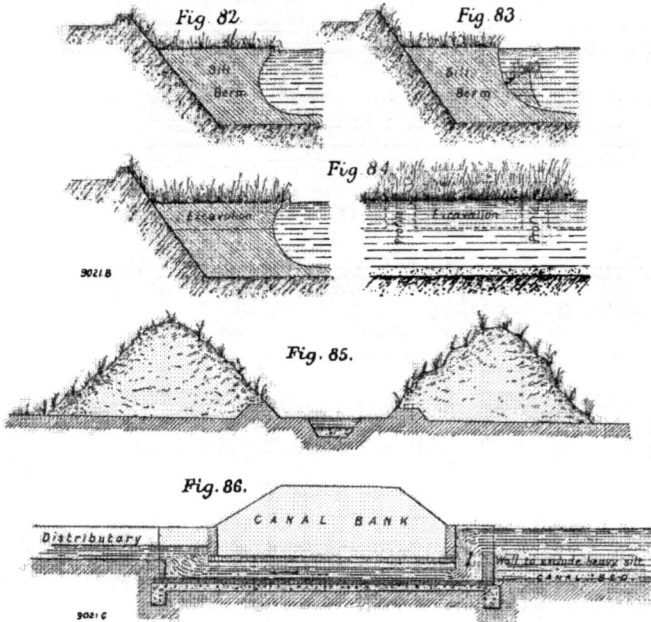

Fig. 82.

Fig. 83.

Fig. 84.

Fig. 85.

Fig. 86.

moment it enters the reach, and the character of the lining, instead of being fairly uniform, will vary considerably ; the deposit at the head consisting only of pure sand which is anything but impervious to water.

During this process of lining the channel, some alterations will occasionally be found necessary in the crests of the weirs or falls that divide the reaches. When the silt deposit does not cease at a point, if it is desirable for it to do so, we may, by lowering the crest of the weir, give an increased velocity to the current above and so accomplish our object.

The condition of the channel should be now as nearly as possible all that can be theoretically desired, but even under the most favourable circumstances it will require constant attention and looking after, in order to keep it always clean and straight.

The berms, formed by the deposition of silt at the sides of a canal, being of slow growth, and consequently close in texture, will stand at a much steeper slope than the made earth of the banks. Indeed, they have a tendency to overhang, for the grass and jungle grow most prolifically upon the berm ; branches and grass droop over in the water and collect an undue proportion of the particles in suspension, and the section takes the form shown in Fig. 82. This tendency can only be checked by trimming or berm-cutting the edges. When this is neglected great pieces of the berm will break off and slip down into the canal bed (Fig. 83). These slips especially occur when the water surface in the channel is suddenly lowered. The berms are saturated and heavy, and when deprived of the support of the water are unable to sustain their own weight. Owing to this constant accumulation of silt at the upper edges, and the falling in of the banks, if berm-cutting is systematically neglected, the whole character of the section will be changed. Gradually becoming narrower and deeper, the channel will also become more and more tortuous. It has now assumed the character of a river, but being in embankment instead of in a valley it has not a river's capacity for taking a flood supply, and when a flood occurs, as it sometimes will do in the best regulated canal, it will burst the banks and flood the country.

The growth of the berms is very insidious, and berm-cutting is an operation that is apt to be overlooked ; it costs money and makes no show for it. When it is remembered that the berm clay forms an excellent material for repairs and for dressing the driving road which is usually found on a canal bank, there should be no excuse whatever for the neglect.

The engineer is sometimes liable to err on the other side. He cuts out great pieces of the berm with which to repair and strengthen his banks, and so as not to interfere with the section of the channel, he leaves, untouched, strong profiles at intervals (Fig. 84). The gaps thus made contain dead water, and silt up almost immediately. Here there is an inexhaustible supply of earth for the repairs of banks. The operation will be repeated, but with a very different result. This last deposit has been formed rapidly ; it is coarse, and has not the same binding properties of the originally slow-grown berm. If it be used to dress off the top of the bank it will form a bad and heavy roadway.

In the older irrigation systems it is the smaller distributing channels that suffer most from silt deposit. In some cases the bed slope given to the main canal was too great, whilst that of the minor channels was insufficient, with the result that heavy deposits of sand formed in the first few furlongs of every distributary, choking it up and rendering it often impossible to cram a sufficient supply of water over the bar so formed. This sand was not merely silt brought down from the river in floods, but was due in a great measure to the scour taking place at various points in the main canal.

The Old Ganges Canal, near the head where the bed is hard and stony, had a bed slope of 2 ft. per mile ; from the second to the fifth mile the bed slope was $1\frac{1}{2}$ ft. per mile, and thenceforward varied from 1 ft. to $1\frac{1}{4}$ ft. Distributaries were given a slope of about 6 in. in the mile. The heads of distributing channels silted up with great rapidity, and from repeated clearance the channels soon presented the appearance shown in Fig. 85. This silt deposit, being due to a very sudden check of velocity, consists of coarse clean sand, which, when piled up close to the distributary, is to a great extent blown back by the wind or washed in again by the rain.

Supposing one of these small irrigating channels having perhaps a bed width of 8 ft. and a depth of water of $3\frac{1}{2}$ ft., to be silt-cleared at the commencement of an irrigation season, at the

G

end of the season a depth of perhaps 2½ ft. of silt will have accumulated in the first furlong, somewhat less in the second, and only about 9 in. at the end of the first mile. Close to the head the deposit is clean white sand, which gradually gets more clayey as it goes on, until, in the second mile, it is quite sticky mud. If the channel be left alone for another season, the deposit will not increase in the same proportion; there will only be found an additional deposit of a few inches, and this of very fine clay. The bed slope thus formed, a gradually decreasing one is evidently the form that should be adopted, and instead of clearing out quantities of sand year after year, we must take measures to raise the water surface in the canal, so as to give a sufficient command of the now elevated distributary bed.

Again, the amount of silt entering from the main canal should be reduced, and as the heavy silt travels along close to the bottom, this may be accomplished to a great extent by taking the supply for the distributary from the surface and not from any great depth. Many of the old distributary heads were designed to take water from the very bottom of the canal, even though the bed of the distributary might be considerably above the canal bed (Fig. 86). An improvement has been made in these by building a low wall across the mouth of the outlet.

In this respect the rough old-fashioned method of regulating a distributary head by dropping planks into grooves is vastly superior to that of employing sluice gates that lift up and allow the water to pass beneath. A system of double sluice gates, the lower of which is generally left down, is now employed with success.

We must, however, go deeper to the root of the evil, if we hope to deal successfully with the question of silt in minor channels. We must endeavour to minimise the quantity of coarse silt in the main canal itself. The principle just mentioned should be applied to the head of the canal, and the surface water only of the river be permitted to enter. The slope of the canal must be reduced in places where there is any tendency to scour; for it is this scour that mainly tends to throw such a quantity of silt on to the lower reaches.

The arrangements in the Lower Ganges Canal, which is of recent construction, for the disposal of silt after it has entered the canal, are very complete. The slope is not very excessive, so that there is no tendency to scour, and most of the coarse sand is deposited in the first two miles. About the second mile there is an escape running back into the Ganges, and the head of this is provided with deep scouring sluices. When these are opened they draw out an immense volume of water, and a sufficient quantity can be admitted at the head to flush the first two miles and drive the sand through the sluices into the Ganges. Lower down the canal the banks are double and the space between is gradually being silted up with good soil.

In the Old Ganges Canal the bed has undergone great changes. In many places the bed has been scoured out into great holes and the silt carried down to the terminal branches. At the tail of the Etawah branch the bed has been raised by these deposits about 4 ft., and the arch openings of the bridges are almost entirely submerged. Of course, were any injury likely to arise from this raising of the bed, it would have been checked long ago; but it is rather an advantage than otherwise, as a much better command of the country is gained than was originally anticipated. Some of the holes in the Ganges Canal bed have become filled up again with coarse sand, and the introduction of weirs or the raising the crests of existing falls has done away with the scour.

With the experience gained from the old Ganges Canal it has been possible to design the irrigation system of the Lower Ganges, so that the distributing channels scarcely ever require alteration. After it has been found that they run successfully for a few seasons and have a good command of the country, that no scour takes place, and that there is no undue deposit of silt, they are rendered as permanent as possible. Masonry bed forms to preserve the bed levels are introduced at every furlong, and the masonry heads of the irrigation outlets act as profiles, so that the repairing and clearing of the channel require very little supervision to see that it is done correctly. The outlets are provided with steps running down from the top of the bank to the distributary bed. These steps, being each 1 ft. in height, serve to gauge the depth of water, and the inspecting officer as he rides along the bank can see at a glance whether his supply is what it ought to be at every point of the distributary. Great care must be taken to see that the outlets are constructed with absolute accuracy, for water is a terrible tell tale, not only as regards strength, but also as regards accuracy of level and alignment. It is one of the

Fig. 87.

severest shocks an engineer can experience after he has lavished the greatest care on the construction of say ten miles of masonry outlets for a canal distributary, to find, when the water is let in again, that each outlet as he comes to it, sticks up higher, or not so high, out of the water as the last, with an irregularity that proves them at once absolutely valueless as water gauges. This is an experience which it is perhaps as well for an engineer to suffer once in his lifetime. He is scarcely likely to allow it to occur a second time.

Next to silt the most troublesome enemies the irrigation channels possess are the weeds. There are two classes of weeds that infest the canals of the Do-āb, called respectively "sirwāl" and "kai;" the former name includes all the weeds that grow upon the bottom, the latter is a floating weed that derives its nourishment from the water and grows as it floats along. If not carefully attended to these weeds can so choke up a channel that it cannot discharge a quarter of its proper volume. The "kai" is particularly dangerous, as it stops up the bridges and syphons, and is very liable to cause breaches in the banks above. During their worst season a staff of men have to be kept employed with rakes and hooks to keep the smaller channels clear. Water weeds may to a great extent be kept down by only permitting the channels to run in alternate weeks; during the dry week, even if the weeds do not die down, they can be very quickly removed by hand. Allowing water heavily charged with silt into the channels has a very good effect, but it is doubtful whether the quantity of the silt deposited more than counterbalances the good done. The wider channels and main canals are cleared by dragging a chain along the bottom up stream as the weeds have a considerable inclination in the direction of the current they are nicely caught by the chain and dragged out of the ground. A number of spiky bamboos attached to the chain add considerably to its efficiency. Sometimes as many as thirty men are employed on each end of the chain. Numerous attempts have been made to design some economical and efficient machine for clearing the weed, but where labour is so cheap, the old-fashioned and simple method has been found the best and most economical. India is a country into which mechanical contrivances intended to supplant manual labour should only be introduced after the most careful thought and experiment. As it is, a very great proportion of the population is employed in doing absolutely nothing for many months in the year and for many hours every day; the introduction of agricultural machinery will deprive the labouring classes, the coolies, of the employment out of which they make their livelihood, weeding, digging, and reaping; honest simple occupations in which the women and children can join with their husbands and brothers; occupations that foster a kindly and friendly disposition towards each other and to strangers. Any one having a knowledge of the Hindoos and Mahommedans of the cities, would feel very sorry to see the simple agriculturists driven to earn their living in grimy factories and squalid alleys. It is a consolation that the smallness of the holdings almost precludes the possibility of the introduction of agricultural machinery and the displacement of the rural population. Even in England it is only on the larger farms that machinery is used to any great extent, and it has been found in recent years that these do not pay so well as the smaller holdings on which hand labour is employed.

In the foregoing articles the author has endeavoured to indicate the main practical points to be carefully considered before undertaking to supply an extensive tract of country with a complete system of irrigation. The points taken up and discussed have been those alone which experience has shown that a canal projector, who has not had many years' experience of the practical working of irrigation systems, would possibly—nay, very probably—misjudge or overlook altogether. They appear simple and obvious when pointed out, but the numerous defects in the old canals of the Do-āb upon which an immense deal of thought and care were expended, show how impossible it is, without experience either personal or second-hand, to foresee all the contingencies that will arise and which should be provided against.

The questions touched upon are only a small portion of the subject. The questions of manuring, deep ploughing, timber growing, the reclamation of waste lands, the introduction of new and suitable crops, water carriage, and many other such questions, demand the attention of the agricultural engineer in addition to the purely engineering points mentioned at the commencement of this article.

The author hopes at some future date to be able to discuss some of these subjects in detail.

PRINTED AT THE BEDFORD PRESS, 20 & 21, BEDFORDBURY, LONDON, W.C.

www.ingramcontent.com/pod-product-compliance
Lightning Source LLC
Chambersburg PA
CBHW031440270326
41930CB00007B/798